GENERAL APTITUDE TESTS

General Aptitude Tests are given for the following reasons:

1. To see how well a child can carry out written instructions.

2. To measure powers of verbal reasoning.

3. To measure powers of numerical reasoning.

4. To measure pure vocabulary.

5. To measure spelling ability.

6. To measure vocabulary associated with general knowledge.

7. To measure spatial and visual ability when presented with diagrams.

8. To measure the speed with which a child can think. This is done by setting more questions within a time limit than can normally be answered correctly.

General Aptitude Tests are similar to Intelligence Quotient (IQ) tests in that they do <u>not</u> measure:

1. Thinking abilities that require physical coordination.

2. The ability to memorise and reproduce facts.

3. Creative ability.

4. Emotional attitudes.

Most children become nervous at the thought of taking IQ or General Aptitude Tests. By practising these papers and therefore encountering a wide variety of the kinds of questions asked, this nervousness should disappear.

Other books published by Coroneos Publications and compiled by Peter Howard which give other examples of General Aptitude Tests questions are:

- Selective/Schools Scholarship Tests – item 64; Years 5–8

- Basic Skills Learn to Think Levels 1 and 2 – items 70, 71; Years 2–6, 5–8

- IQ Examples Levels 1 and 2 – items 154,155; Years 3–4, 5–8

- Further Selective Schools/Scholarships Tests – item 112; Years 5–8

- Year 3 Basic Skills Tests – item 144

- Year 4 Opportunity Class Tests – item 125

- Year 5 Basic Skills Tests – item 153

- Preparation for Selective School/Scholarship Tests – item 404, 405, 406 for Years 3–4, 4–5, 5–8 respectively.

Even if children do not wish to prepare for Selective Schools, Entrance or Scholarship Examinations, they will enjoy the challenge of working out the answers in all these books. By taking note of mistakes made, their general mental capacity must improve.

(1)   State the correct meaning of the word LURID.

(A   GLOWING AND FIERY.   (B) CLEAR   (C) LED AWAY   (D) DANGEROUS

(2)   The number that comes next in the series 1 5 9 13 .... is

(A) 17   (B) 14   (C) 15   (D) 16

(3)   ANGINA is a disease that causes pain in the .... The correct answer is

(A) FOOT   (B) HEAD   (C) HEART   (D) EAR

(4)   Bicaster is smaller than Gatley. Manchester is larger than Upton. Upton is larger than Gatley. Which of the towns is the largest?

(A)   Upton   (B) Manchester   (C) Gatley   (D) Bicaster

(5)   State the figure that comes next in sequence:

(A)   (B)   (C)   (D)

(6)   Donna went on an afternoon TV quiz show called 'Twenty Questions'. She was given $3 for each question she answered correctly and had to pay back $2 for each question she had wrong. After answering 20 questions Donna had neither won nor lost money. How many questions had she answered correctly?
6   8   10   12   14   16   18

(7)   Use all the letters from the word LEARNT to make
something of which a male deer has two.   ....

(8)   ICE is to SOLID as STEAM is to:

(A) WATER   (B) BOIL   (C) HEAT   (D) GAS

(9)   My niece would be my:

(A) brother's wife   (B) father's sister   (C) brother's daughter (D) sister's son

(10)   What word is similar in meaning to the word CALAMITY?

      (A) INSULT   (B) DISCOVERY   (C) STILLNESS (D) DISASTER

Only one word of each pair is spelt correctly. State the correct one.

(11)   entrence entrance   (12) archery archary   (13) audable audible

---

(14)   If all the vowels were taken out of the alphabet, which would then be the 18th letter?

      (A) Y   (B) Z   (C) U   (D) W

---

(15)   State the number in the problem which is not needed to solve it.

At the supermarket I bought 4 packets of biscuits at $1.35 each and paid with a $10 note. How much did I pay for the biscuits?

Complete the word in each sentence by adding three letters. These three letters make up a word. Write the word again as an answer.

Shopkeepers are in business to make a pro.........................   (16) ....

The teacher said there was no exc................... for being late. (17) ....

I do not int.............. to make a mistake.   (18) ....

---

(19)   If the word UNCLE is written in code as VODMF, what would DIFFTF be? ....

Look carefully at the sentence and find the hidden fruit. Write it as an answer.

The area was known as Camp Lumberjack because many timber cutters lived there.   (20) ....

From our boat we saw two natives grab an anaconda that was swimming near to the shore.   (21) ....

---

(22)   State the odd word in the group. (A) parsnip (B) pomegranate (C) leek (D) onion

---

(23)   State the one word which names the class to which the others belong.

      (A) nylon   (B) calico   (C) material   (D) cotton

---

(1)   The correct meaning of the word PITTANCE is

   (A) FIGHT BETWEEN TWO PEOPLE   (B) A SMALL ALLOWANCE OF MONEY
   (C) CONFESSION   (D) DESERVING PITY

(2)   What number comes next in the series?   3   6   12   24   ....

   (A) 18   (B) 38   (C) 64   (D) 48

(3)   If a person had a cataract, he or she might need an operation on the ....

   (A) foot   (B) eye   (C) ear   (D) heart

(4)   Stewart Brown goes to primary school with his two sisters and three brothers. His
      father's brother has three daughters at the same school. If both parents are alive, how
      many are there altogether in the two families with the surname Brown?

   8   9   10   11   12   13   14

(5)   Circle the figure that comes next in sequence:

   (A)   (B)   (C)   (D)

(6)   Dad wanted his car to be clean and shiny every day for a week to impress a customer of
      his. To hose and wipe down the car, he offered to pay his son James 15 cents the first
      day and double the daily payment each succeeding day thereafter. If James accepted
      the deal, how much money did he make?
   $9.60 $12.40 $14.40 $16.20 $19.05 $38.25

(7)   Use all the letters from the word FLIERS to make weapons
      that are used by soldiers.   ....

(8)   ENEMY is to HOSTILE as ALLY is to F.............

(9)   Shoes used for walking or sport all have:

   (A) laces   (B) straps   (C) rubber   (D) soles

(10)   State the word that is similar in meaning to the word EDIFICE.

    (A) BUILDING   (B) CANCEL   (C) LACKING   (D) JOURNALIST

Only one word of each pair is spelt correctly. State the correct one.

(11) docter doctor   (12) fragrent fragrant   (13) gorgeous gorgious

---

(14)   Make a word using letters from both words below, that are not in both.
        (Note: repeated letters are counted separately).

        CHEATERS   SCATHED   ....

---

(15)   Circle the number in the problem which is not needed to solve it.

        *In our class there are 34 desks and we have 13 girls and 19 boys. How many
        more boys are there than girls?*

Complete the word in each sentence by adding three letters. These three letters make up a
word. Write the word again as an answer.

Autumn is a pleasant sea ………….. in Sydney.   (16) ....

It is hard to comp……past champion tennis players with those of today. (17) ....

The serv ……. and the food in the restaurant were excellent.   (18) ....

---

(19) If the word GOLDEN is written in code as IQNFGP, what would TQDDGT be? ....

Look carefully at the sentence and find the hidden fish. Write it as an answer.

The telegram read: 'Be at Universal Monday morning at nine'.   (20) ....

I saw a Pfaff lathe advertised in the local paper yesterday.   (21) ....

---

(22)   State the odd word in the group. (A) ling   (B) bass   (C) finch   (D) snook

---

(23)   State the one word which names the class to which the others belong.

        (A) stone   (B) granite   (C) marble   (D) slate

---

(1) The correct meaning of the word RAUCOUS is

   (A) WILD   (B) EXCITED
   (C) HOARSE OR HARSH SOUNDING   (D) BADLY BEHAVED

(2) What number comes next in the series? 5 8 12 17 ....

   (A) 23   (B) 22   (C) 26   (D) 25

(3) People who have jaundice turn a ....colour. State the right answer.

   (A) blue   (B) red   (C) pale   (D) yellow

(4) Mr Rider has stables on his property that are numbered from 1 to 6. The odd numbered stables are for his mares and the rest for his geldings. In the first two he keeps brown horses. In numbers 3 and 4 are the black horses. In the other two are grey horses. The horses in the even numbered stables are all small so that children can ride them. In which stable is the large brown mare?

   1 2 3 4 5 6

(5) Circle the figure that comes next in sequence

   (A)   (B)   (C)   (D)

(6) Using only 5c, 10c and 20c coins, how many ways can you arrange them so that they total 35c?

   2   3   4   5   6   7   8   9

(7) Use all the letters of the word ANGERED to make a small military weapon. ....

(8) COAL is to MINE as STONE is to ....

State the correct word in the brackets.

(9) I bought envelopes in the (stationery   stationary) store.

(10) The school (principal   principle) laid a wreath on Anzac Day.

(11)   State the word that is similar in meaning to the word SCOLD.

     (A) REVEAL   (B) REBUKE   (C) RETARD   (D) RESOLVE

Only one word of each pair is spelt correctly. State the correct one.

(12)   bycicle bicycle   (13) disappear dissappear (14) propellor propeller

---

(15)   Write the first five letters of the alphabet which, when written in capitals, have only have straight lines.

      ....

---

(16)   Four children sit at a square table playing cards. The girls Sue and Judy are on opposite sides of the table. Jack is on Sue's left. Who is on Tim's right?

     (A) Sue   (B) Jack   (C) Judy   (D) Not enough information given

---

Complete the word in each sentence by adding three letters. These three letters make up a word. Write the word again as an answer.

The general laid a wreath at the unkn.............. soldier's tomb.   (17) ....

One state occasions the Queen rides in her carri.............. .   (18) ....

The old mansion was a bargain but they will have to redecor......... .
some rooms.   (19) ....

To make this sentence sensible, cross out one word and write one that rhymes with it.

Robin Hood and his men lived in a shady blade deep in Sherwood Forest. (20) ....

Look carefully at the sentence and find the hidden farm animal. Write it as an answer.

She left a message to say that she had to go at noon tomorrow.   (21) ....

Mum left us some sandwiches so we would not be hungry.   (22) ....

---

(23)   State the odd word in the group. (A) aphid   (B) lynx   (C) gnat (D) louse

---

(24)   State the word which names the class to which the others belong.

     (A) diamond   (B) sapphire   (C) ruby   (D) gem

---

(1) State the correct meaning of the word FALLACY.

(A) STUPIDITY   (B) VIVID DREAM   (C) A MISTAKEN IDEA   (D) HESITATION

(2) Circle the number that comes next in the series?   0.3   0.5   0.7   0.9 ....

(A) 1.0   (B) 0.01   (C) 0.1   (D) 1.1

(3) A person who suffers from insomnia would be unable to: ....

(A) think   (B) sleep   (C) walk   (D) eat

(4) Mr Watson has three dogs – a spaniel, a Doberman and a kelpie. Neither Sam nor Digger is the Doberman. Digger is the oldest of the dogs and is friends with the kelpie. What is the kelpie's name?

(A) Willy   (B) Sam   (C) Digger   (D) not enough information to determine it.

(5) Solve the relationship between the figures: ◯ is to ◯ as △ is to

(A) ◯   (B) ∘   (C) ◿   (D) ▭

(6) Mum cut 8 roses from her garden. She had two vases – one tall and the other shallow. If she put at least one rose in each vase, how many different combinations of roses could she have in the two vases altogether?

5   6   7   8   9   10

The missing word must be made from all the letters of the word in bold.

(7) *Before the **battle** began, the tank commander took a ....to calm his nerves.*

(8) SET is to DISHES as CANTEEN is to .... (Use one word for the answer)

(9) State the correct word: *For (dessert   desert) I had plum pudding and ice cream.*

(10)   State the word that is similar in meaning to the word AUTHORITY.

(A) SENIORITY   (B) JUSTIFICATION   (C) JURISDICTION   (D) APPLICATION

Only one word of each pair is spelt correctly. State the correct one.

(11)   occurred ocurred   (12) moveble   movable   (13) government goverment

---

(14)   Write the fourth letter of the alphabet which when written in capitals, would look the same if it was seen in a mirror.   ....

---

(15)   If you set out very early in the morning by car and you were travelling due West, through which window would the Sun be shining at the beginning of the trip?

(A) front   (B) back   (C) left-side   (D) right-side

Complete the word in each sentence by adding three letters. These three letters make up a word. Write the word again as an answer.

Every restaurant must have a kitc......... .   (16) ....

An ignor...... person knows less than someone who is educated.   (17) ....

China is planning to build a huge dam to irrig...... vast tracts of land.   (18) ....

To make this sentence sensible, cross out one word and write one that rhymes with it.

The motorist hoped he would not be booked as he was in a no parking cone. (19) ....

Look carefully at the sentence and find the hidden vegetable. Write it as an answer.

The old farmer became too old to drive and let his car rot in the shed.   (20) ....

We camped in a pretty spot at Oberon where there is a dam full of trout.   (21) ....

---

(22)   State the odd word in the group. (A) prostrate (B) level (C) smooth (D) undulating

---

(23)   State the word meaning the opposite of the other three:

(A) discover   (B) mislay   (C) observe   (D) detect

---

(1) State the correct meaning of the word PROFOUND.

(A) DISCOVERED   (B) DEAF   (C) VERY DEEP   (D) PLENTIFUL

(2) State the number that comes next in the series? 1.20 0.60 0.30 0.15 ....

(A) 0.2   (B) 0   (C) 0.5   (D) 0.075   (E) 0.75

(3) A person who suffers from indigestion probably has ....

(A) gangrene   (B) arthritis   (C) migraine   (D) dyspepsia

(4) James, Olga and George each prefers one of the following sports; tennis, golf and swimming. James finds swimming boring. George detests ball games. Olga is always on the court looking for someone to have a hit. Who likes golf?

(A) James   (B) Olga   (C) George   (D) insufficient information given to decide.

(5) Solve the relationship between the figures. �__ is to ▬ as ◣ is to

(A)  ☐   (B)  ◣   (C)  ◿   (D) 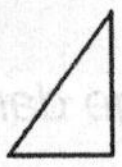 ◺

(6) The average of a batsman's last four innings was 19. If he scored 28, 16 and 32 in the first three innings, what was his score in the last one?

0 2 4 6 8 10 12

The missing word must be made from all the letters of the word in bold.

(7) In the **garden** there is always the .... of being bitten by a funnel web spider.

(8) MERCER is to CLOTH as MILLINER is to .... *(Use one word for the answer.)*

State the correct word.

(9) The (guerilla gorilla) is an intelligent animal.

(10) It was a (sheer shear) drop from the window to the street below.

(11) What word is similar in meaning to the word BALMY.

(A) CRAZY   (B) MILD   (C) WILD   (D) PICTURESQUE

Only one word of each pair is spelt correctly. State the correct one.

(12) skilful skillful   (13) parrallel parallel   (14) possess posess

(15) If the alphabet was written backwards, which letter would be number 8 in line? ....
....

(16) Timothy is standing to attention in the playground and is facing north east. If he makes an about turn, in which direction is he now facing?

(A) north west   (B) south east   (C) north east   (D) south west

Complete the word in each sentence by adding three letters. These three letters make up a word. Write the word again as an answer.

The slip fielder took a splen....... catch with the back of his hand on the grass. (17) ....

The mountaineer stumb...... and fell to his death down a crevasse.   (18) ....

Dark clouds began to threa..... so the lights of the stadium were switched on. (19) ....

To make this sentence sensible, cross out one word and write one that rhymes with it.

Distances between towns by air are often spoken of as how far the snow flies. (20) ....

Look carefully at the sentence and find an animal of the cat family. Write it as an answer.

We are leaving for a holiday to Bali on the following Saturday.   (21) ....

Mr Bahaja guarantees that any jewellery he sells cannot be bought cheaper. (22) ....

(23) State the odd word in the group. (A) kerosene (B) diesel (C) nitrogen (D) petroleum

(24) State the word which names the class to which the others belong.

(A) rice   (B) oats   (C) cereal   (D) wheat

(1)   State the correct meaning of the word DELIRIOUS.

   (A) WILDLY EXCITED OR FEVERISH   (B) CARRYING AND HANDLING OF GOODS
   (C) AN OFFENDER   (D) NOT REAL

(2)   What is the number that comes next in the series? 2.4   1.2   0.6   0.3   ....

   (A) 0.15   (B) 0.1   (C) 0.2   (D) 0

Write the missing word from each proverb.

(3)   *A drowning man will clutch at a ....*   (4) *Actions speak louder than ....*

(5)   *Don't put all your .... in one basket.*

(6)   Five horses take part in a race. Lucky beat Star but could not catch Brumby. Shorty
      was left behind by Bozo but managed to beat Brumby. Which horse came last?

   (A) Star   (B) Lucky   (C) Brumby   (D) Shorty   (E) Bozo

(7)   Solve the relationship between the figures.

(8)   Six tennis players enter for a round robin tournament in which each player has one
      match against every other player. How many matches would be played to complete the
      tournament?
      10   12   14   15   16   18

The missing word must be made from all the letters of the word in bold.

(9)   *Mum bought two **plates** and a cup for baby Anne in the .... of pink shades.*

(10) CONVENT is to NUN as MONASTERY is to ....

State the correct word.

(11) *That building is fifteen (stories   storeys) high.*

(12) *Iron (oar   ore) is mined in Western Australia.*

(13)   State the word that is similar in meaning to the word GAUDY.

(A) WEALTHY   (B) GREEDY   (C) CAREFUL   (D) SHOWY

Only one word of each pair is spelt correctly. State the correct one.

(14)   gaurd   guard   (15) handkerchief hankerchief   (16) immediately immediatly

---

(17)   How many vowels are there in the second half of the alphabet?   ....

---

(18)   Timothy is standing to attention in the playground and is facing south west. If he turns
left through 90º, in which direction is he now facing?

(A) north west   (B) south east   (C) north east   (D) south west

---

Complete the word in each sentence by adding three letters. These three letters make up a
word. Write the word again as an answer.

To tresp....... means to enter someone's property without permission.   (19) ....

Fem............. turtles leave the sea to lay eggs in sand near the water's edge. (20) ....

It is an advant....... to practise these examples before sitting for an aptitude test. (21) ....

To make this sentence sensible, cross out one word and write one that rhymes with it.

A foal is an animal that burrows and lives under the ground.   (22) ....

Look carefully at the sentence and find a reptile. Write it as an answer.

My grandfather still swims naked in his private pool every night about ten o'clock. (23) ....

---

(24)   State the odd word in the group.

(A) Greenland   (B) Samoa   (C) Nepal   (D) Tierra del Fuego

---

(25)   State the word which names the class to which the others belong.

(A) mineral   (B) iron   (C) silver   (D) lead

---

(1) State the correct meaning of the word GESTICULATE.

(A) CHEW NOISILY   (B) TALK QUICKLY
(C) MAKE SIGNS WITH THE HANDS   (D) OFFER TO DO SOMETHING

(2) Circle the number that comes next in the series? 60 50 120 110 180 ....

(A) 160   (B) 170   (C) 240   (D) 190   (E) 200

(3) If a person had a disease of the larynx, it would affect his or her ....

(A) walking   (B) digestion   (C) hearing   (D) speech

Write the missing word from each proverb.

(4) *A barking dog never ....*   (5) *A rolling stone gathers no ....*

(6) *Curiosity killed the ....*

(7) Three girls each had a different coloured ball. Firstly, Denise threw her red ball to Simone who at the same time threw her blue ball to Denise. Denise then threw her ball to Marcia who threw her green ball back to Denise. Lastly, Simone and Marchia threw their balls to each other. Who then held the red ball?

(A) Denise   (B) Simone   (C) Marcia   (D) Insufficient information given

(8) Solve the relationship between the figures.

(9) Walter's parents offered him $10 every time he passed his weekly spelling test at school. However, if he failed he was to pay them $7.50. At the end of the school year, which consisted of 4 twelve-week terms, Walter had made $270. How many times did Walter fail his weekly test?
8 9 10 11 12 13 14 15

The missing word must be made from all the letters of the word in bold.

(10) *The chef had no idea what could* **cause** *the .... he made to have a bitter taste.*

(11)   State the word that is similar in meaning to the word OUTSET.

    (A) EXIT   (B) END   (C) BEGINNING   (D) BEYOND

Only one word of each pair is spelt correctly. State the correct one.

(12)   woolen   woollen   (13) buried   burried   (14) beutiful   beautiful

---

(15)   In the word AUTOGRAPH, which letter is nearest to the middle of the alphablet? ....

---

(16)   Take five letters away from PURPOSELY to make a flower.   ....

(17)   Take eight letters away from CONGLOMERATE to make an animal.   ....

Complete the word in each sentence by adding three letters. These three letters make up a word. Write the word again as an answer.

In public pools it is forbidden to ba....... without wearing swimwear.   (18) ....

There was some de .... until the aircraft was cleared for take- off .   (19) ....

Satellite navigation enables ships to know their ex .... position at sea.   (20) ....

To make this sentence sensible, cross out one word and write one that rhymes with it.

The pilot flew low and boomed over the airfield.   (21) ....

Look carefully at the sentence and find an Australian state. Write it as an answer.

The government sent Mr Petrovic to Riad in Saudi Arabia.   (22) ....

---

(23)   State the odd word in the group.

    (A) Pacific   (B) Tasman   (C) Danube   (D) Caspian   (E) Atlantic

---

(24)   State the word that rhymes with ski:

    (A) whey   (B) vie   (C) quay   (D) neigh

---

(1)   State the correct meaning of the word BEQUEATH.

    (A) ANCIENT WORD MEANING 'UNDER'   (B) UNDER WATER
    (C) LEAVE LONELY BY DEATH   (D) GIVE WHEN ONE DIES

(2)   Circle the fraction that comes next in the series? $\frac{1}{2}$ $\frac{3}{5}$ $\frac{7}{10}$ $\frac{4}{5}$ ....

    (A) $\frac{3}{4}$ (B) $1\frac{1}{5}$ (C) 1   (D) $\frac{9}{10}$

(3)   A person who sees a doctor for an aural complaint has trouble with his or her ....

    (A) ears   (B) mouth   (C) eyes   (D) brain

Write the missing word from each proverb.

(4)   *A watched pot never* ....   (5) *Beggars can't be* ....

(6)   *Every cloud has a silver* ....

(7)   Four children are in the front row in class facing the teacher. The teacher sees Donald on her left, Helen next, Martin next, and June on the right. When the teacher goes out of the room, Donald changes places with Martin and then Martin changes places with Helen. Who is now on Donald's right?

    (A) Martin   (B) Helen   (C) June   (D) Not enough information given.

(8)   Solve the relationship between the figures. is to as is to

    (A)   (B)   (C)   (D)

(9)   Three members of the Ferrari racing team entered a one-lap race. They were Sergio, Davies and Muntz. The three drivers took the first three places. They were so close together that a camera decided the placings. How many different combinations of placings were possible?

    3 6 9 12 15

The missing word must be made from all the letters of the word in bold.

(10)   Naomi **dreads** walking in the long grass as two .... were seen on a rock sunning themselves before slithering away.

(11)   State the word that is similar in meaning to the word ENTREAT.

    (A) RETREAT   (B) SURPRISE   (C) BEG   (D) GIVE

Only one word of each pair is spelt correctly. State the correct one.

(12)   rythm   rhythm   (13) adress address   (14) billious   bilious

(15)   In the word 'FEDERATION' there are three letters that come together in the alphabet. Write them.   ....

(16)   Take four letters away from THROBBING to make a bird.   ....

(17)   Take five letters away from CASTANET to make a tiny creature.   ....

Complete the word in each sentence by adding four letters.   These four letters make up a word. Write the word again as an answer.

A computer is made up of a sy................ of silicon chips.   (18) ....

Malaria is a tropical dis........... that is spread by the mosquito.   (19) ....

There is always the likeli.......... that you can have an accident in a car.   (20) ....

To make this sentence sensible, cross out one word and write one that rhymes with it.

The hive was a dance that became popular in the 1940's.   (21) ....

Look carefully at the sentence and find the largest Australian lake. Write it as an answer.

At Gallipoli Simpson and his donkey rescued many wounded soldiers.   (22) ....

(23)   State the odd word in the group. (A) catalogue (B) calendar (C) atlas (D) novel

(24)   State the word that rhymes with suede: (A) feud (B) crude (C) weighed (D) freed

(1)   State the correct meaning of the word GRANDEUR.

(A) BOASTING   (B) LITTLE BY LITTLE
(C) SPANISH NOBLEMAN   (D) GREATNESS AND SPLENDOUR

(2)   State the letter below that comes next in the series.   C E C F C

(A) H   (B) F   (C) G   (D) I

(3)   An asthmatic person has trouble ....

(A) speaking.   (B) breathing.   (C) walking.   (D) sleeping.

Write the missing word from each proberb.

(4)   *A stitch in time saves* ....   (5) *He who hesitates is* ....

(6)   *Look before you* ....

(7)   A scientist was working with some microbes that she knew divided in two every two and
a half minutes. She placed one of these microbes on a glass slide under a microscope
at 10 a.m. How many of these microbes would she be able to see at 10.30 a.m.?

(A) 512   (B) 1024   (C) 2048   (D) 4096   (E) 8192

(8)   Solve the relationship between the figures.

(A) ⊙   (B) ◯▲   (C) ◯⊙   (D) ◯⊙

(9)   Julie, Sophie, Megan, Jan and Pat took part in the final of the 100 metres race. Jan ran
faster than Sophie but did not come first. Pat did not come last. There was only one
person behind Julie, Megan beat Pat. Who came fourth?

(A) Julie   (B) Sophie   (C) Megan   (D) Jan   (E) Pat

The missing word must be made from all the letters of the word in bold.

(10)   *Elias and his bride made a charming couple as they walked down the* .... *of the*
church.

(11)   What word does the middle letter of the abbreviation D.F.C. stand for? ....

(12)   State the word that is similar in meaning to the word TARDY.

      (A) SLOW   (B) MESSY   (C) STRONG   (D) ANNOYED

Only one word of each pair is spelt correctly. State the correct one.

(13)   February Febuary   (14) cemetry cemetery   (15) Wensday Wednesday

(16)   How many more consonants are there than vowels in the name CONSTANTINOPLE?

          ....

(17)   Take seven letters away from IMAGINATION to make a tiny insect.   ....

(18)   Take nine letters away from COMPATIBILITY to make an Australian gemstone. ....

Complete the word in each sentence by adding four letters. These four letters make up a word.
Write the word again as an answer.

A car is protected against hail damage by keeping it in a carport or ga…….. .   (19)...............

In a referendum people can op…….. a proposal by voting against it.   (20) ....

Another name for a wife or hus……. is a spouse.   (21) ....

To make this sentence sensible, cross out one word and write one that rhymes with it.

A jealous person is one who is keen and works hard.   (22)................

(23)   Which word is not like the other three?

      (A) general   (B) colonel   (C) admiral   (D) brigadier

(24)   State the word that means the opposite of the other three.

      (A) bungling   (B) prudent   (C) tactful   (D) diplomatic

(25)   State the word that rhymes with debris:

      (A) eye   (B) tree   (C) hiss   (D) fizz

(1)   State the correct meaning of the word FISSURE.

     (A) A SPLIT OR CRACK   (B) SOMETHING THAT CANNOT BE MOVED
     (C) ABOUNDING IN FISH   (D) CERTAIN

---

(2)   Circle the number that comes next in the series?   64   49   36   25   …………

     (A) 20   (B) 18   (C) 16   (D) 12   (E) 10

---

(3)   On what part of the body is a person most likely to have a bunion?

     (A) head   (B) knee   (C) hand   (D) foot

Write the missing word from each proverb.

(4)   *Once bitten, twice …………* .   (5) *Strike while the iron is …………* .

(6)   *Spare the rod and spoil the …………* .

---

(7)   Mrs Simmons has 1 pair of white, 1 pair of green, 2 pairs of grey and 4 pairs of brown gloves. They are all the same brand and pattern. She keeps them all jumbled up in her bottom drawer. What is the least number of gloves Mrs Simmons should take out of the drawer in the dark to be sure she had a matching pair?

     2   3   4   5   6   7   8

---

(8)   Which one of the figures is odd or different from the other four?

     (A)   (B)   (C)   (D)   (E)

---

(9)   Three housewives with children lived at numbers 19, 21 and 23 in a street. Their husbands were home at week-ends. The lady in 19 shopped on Wednesdays. The lady in 21 shopped every week-day except Tuesday and Friday. The lady in 23 shopped on Monday and alternate week-days after that. On which day would these three houses be vulnerable to a burglary?

     Monday   Tuesday   Wednesday   Thursday   Friday   Saturday   Sunday

---

The missing word must be made from all the letters of the word in bold.

(10)   *My hairdresser always cuts my **fringe** one …………… width from my eyebrows.*

---

(11)   What word does the middle letter of the abbreviation H.R.H. stand for? ....

(12)   State the word that is similar in meaning to the word DUBIOUS.

    (A) HORRIBLE   (B) DIRTY   (C) DOUBTFUL   (D) SHINING

Only one word of each pair is spelt correctly. State the correct one.

(13)   umberella umbrella   (14) unconscious unconcious   (15) forty fourty

(16)   What month begins with the 15th letter of the alphabet? ....

(17)   HORSE is to NEIGH as ELEPHANT is to ....

(18)   BEER is to BREWERY as PETROL is to ....

Complete the word in each sentence by adding four letters. These four letters make up a word.
Write the word again as an answer.

Another name for 'hobby' is pas..........   (19) ....

To pre .... catching some diseases we can be inoculated.   (20) ....

People pro .... outside parliament if they are unhappy about something. (21) ....

To make this sentence sensible, cross out one word and write one that rhymes with it.

There was a long stew for tickets outside the cricket ground before the match. *(22)* ....

(23)   Which word is not like the other three?

    (A) Paris   (B) Moscow   (C) Athens   (D) Belgium

(24)   State the word that means the opposite of the other three.

    (A) destitute   (B) needy   (C) affluent   (D) reduced

(25)   State the word that rhymes with facade:

    (A) braid   (B) caddy   (C) card   (D) Saturday

(1)   State the correct meaning of the word PLAUSIBLE.

(A) PLEASANT   (B) SEEMING TO BE TRUE
(C) PRAISEWORTHY   (D) ABLE TO BE HEARD

---

(2)   State the number that comes next in the series?   5   9   17   33   65   …………

(A) 129   (B) 103   (C) 145   (D) 108   (E) 131

---

(3)   Diabetics build up too much …………….. in their blood. State the right answer.

(A) iron   (B) sugar   (C) salt   (D) calcium

Write the missing colour from each idiom.

(4)   *She was ……………….. with envy.*

(5)   *He sees everything through …………. coloured glasses.*

(6)   *Dad is tickled ……………. with his new car.*

---

(7)   Diana's mother gave her a sum of money (which was divisible by 10) to buy a pair of good running shoes. On passing a sports store she noticed that everything for sale was offered at 25% discount. She was delighted to find that she spent less than she had originally planned. How much were the shoes which Diana bought at the discounted price?

(A) $40   (B) $50   (C) $60   (D) $100

---

(8)   State which one of the figures that is odd or different from the other four.

(A)   (B)   (C)   (D)   (E)

---

(9)   A Mizda, Datsin, Holdin and a Fird took part in a motor race. Each car was painted a different colour. The Fird was white. The Mizda came just behind the black car. The winner was the green car which just beat the black car which was not the Datsin. The Fird came last.

The blue car was the ………………. and it came ………………. .

The missing word must be made from all the letters of the word in bold.

(10) **Among** *the paw paw trees was a single .... tree that bore fruit.*

---

(11)   What word does the middle letter of the abbreviation R.A.N. stand for? ....

---

(12)   State the word that is similar in meaning to the word HALLOWED.

   (A) LEVEL   (B) PLOUGHED   (C) SACRED   (D) VACANT

Only one word of each pair is spelt correctly. State the correct one.

(13)   grammer grammar   (14) jeweller jeweler   (15) sugar suger

---

(16)   How many different letters are there in the word UNCONSTITUTIONAL? ....

---

(17)   ABBATOIR is to MEAT as TANNERY is to ....

(18)   DUCK is to DRAKE as GOOSE is to ....

Complete the word in each sentence by adding four letters. These four letters make up a word.
Write the word again as an answer.

Actors and actresses rehearse before they per .... on stage.   (19)
....

The Prime Minister wants to pro .... a toast to the visiting President.   (20) ....

The sau......... is the most common item of food that is cooked on a barbecue. (21) ....

To make this sentence sensible, cross out one word and write one that rhymes with it.

One clean in the film had to be cut as it was too violent.   (22) ....

---

(23)   Which word is not like the other three? (A) oboe (B) flute (C) saxophone (D) cello

---

(24)   State the word that means the opposite of the other three.

   (A) clemency   (B) harshness   (C) leniency   (D) compassion

---

(25)   State the word that rhymes with wrath: (A) froth (B) bath (C) lathe (D) oath

---

(1) State the correct meaning of the word DESPONDENT.

  (A) LOSE COURAGE OR HOPE   (B) AN INJURED RULER
  (C) A WRITER OF LETTERS   (D) A PERSON WHO IS TRIED IN COURT

(2) State the number that comes next in the series? 1 1 2 3 5 8 13 ......

  17 18 19 20 21 22 23 24

(3) Add 3 letters that make a writing fluid then you have a colour.   p.............

(4) Add 3 letters that make a donkey and you have a word meaning 'to go by'.   p.............

(5) Add 3 letters that make a word meaning 'eaten' and then you have a friend. m.............

Write the missing colour.

(6) David wore a canary .... jumper to golf.

(7) The carpet on the floor was emerald ....

(8) His hands were jet .... after cleaning the old lamp.

(9) A flower grower decided that she needed 287 grams of poppy seeds. The seed supplier
     sold the seeds in 1, 2, 5, 15, 25 and 50 gram packets. What is the least number of
     packets she can buy to fulfil her order?

  6 7 8 9 10 11 12

(10) State which one of the figures that is odd or different from the other four.

  (A)   (B)   (C)   (D)   (E)

(11) Bob and Tim have fair hair. John and Bill have dark hair. Only Tim and Bill are tall. All
     the boys except John wear their hair short. Who is the short dark-haired boy with long
     hair?
     (A) Bob   (B) Tim   (C) John   (D) Bill

The missing word must be made from all the letters of the word in bold.

(12) Dad said it was dishonest to **teach** my brother to .... at cards.

(13)   What word does the middle letter of the abbreviation L.P.G. stand for? ....

(14)   State the word that is similar in meaning to the word PLACID.

(A) ANGRY   (B) TIMID   (C) CALM   (D) RUDE

Only one word of each pair is spelt correctly. State the correct one.

(15)   irritable   irritible   (16) superviser supervisor   (17) oblige oblidge

(18)   In the word DEPOSITED take out all the letters that come next to each other in the
        alphabet. Write any letters that remain.   ....

(19)   STEVEDORE is to CARGO as REMOVALIST is to ....

(20)   BUNCH is to GRAPES as HAND is to ....

Complete the word in each sentence by adding four letters. These four letters make up a word.
Write the word again as an answer.

Another word for street is thorough ....   (21) ....

A submarine is able to travel under water or on the sur ....   (22) ....

Before Christmas, thousands of tur .... are killed and snap frozen.   (23) ....

To make this sentence sensible, cross out one word and write one that rhymes with it.

Pirates were fond of burying their leisure on remote islands.   (24) ....

(25)   Which word is not like the other three?

(A) noxious   (B) foul   (C) florid   (D) rank

(26)   State the word in the brackets that is associated with the word in bold.

Computer   [(A) valves   (B) revolutions   (C) discs   (D) crankshafts]

(27)   State the word that rhymes with sleight.

(A) spite   (B) trait   (C) sleet   (D) float

(1)   State the correct meaning of the word FERVOUR.

(A) TO SEE FIRST   (B) A HIGH BODY TEMPERATURE
(C) KINDNESS   (D) KEENNESS AND ZEAL

(2)   State the number that comes next in the series? 1.75   1.5   1.25   1   ....

(A) 0.075   (B) 0.75   (C) 0.95   (D) 0.095

(3)   Add 3 letters that make unwell then you have a word meaning <u>murder.</u>
      k..............

(4)   Add 3 letters that make request and then you have a <u>covering for your face</u>. m.............

(5)   Add 3 letters that make the remains of a fire and then you have a
      word meaning <u>whip.</u>   ℓ.............

Write the missing colour.   (6)   *A .... letter day is a special one.*

(7) *The curtains were lime ....*   (8)   *She wore a navy .... coat.*

(9)   To fly from Glasgow to London a passenger can take a flight via Liverpool or Manchester
      or Birmingham or Norwich. Then to fly on to Sydney it is possible to go via Bangkok or
      Singapore or Colombo. How many different routes can a person take who flies from
      Glasgow to Sydney?

(A) 12   (B) 16   (C) 18   (D) 24   (E) 30

(10) State the figure that comes next in sequence.

      (A)   (B)   (C)   (D)

(11) A, B, C, D, E and F are six interstate trucks. Only B, D and E are refrigerated and can
      carry perishable goods. If trucks A and C are off the road for repairs, which truck would
      most likely be used to carry a load of wool?

      A   B   C   D   E   F

The missing word must be made from all the letters of the word in bold.

*(12)   To **rescue** the stricken yacht, the police launch had to .... a rope to the stern
      and tow it off the rocks.*

(13)   What word does the middle letter of the abbreviation B.H.P. stand for?   ....

(14)   State the word that is similar in meaning to the word POISED.

   (A) CLIMBED   (B) BALANCED   (C) KILLED   (D) SURPRISED

Only one word of each pair is spelt correctly. State the correct one.

(15)   occasion   ocasion   (16) seperate   separate   (17) enrole   enrol

(18)   In the word IMPONDERABLE, five of its letters come together in the alphabet.
        Write them in alphabetical order.   ....

(19)   BELL is to RING as HINGE is to ....

(20)   KNIFE is to SHEATH as SWORD is to ....

Complete the word in each sentence by adding four letters. These four letters make up a word.
Write the word again as an answer.

A quartz watch driven by a battery is more accu............ than an old one with a spring.
                                                    (21).....................
A person who is extremely unhappy can be described as miser ....   (22) ....
A vegetable with a red skin often used in a salad is the ra ....   (23) ....

To make this sentence sensible, cross out one word and write one that rhymes with it.

A boy who has not yet become a man is a sleuth.   (24) ....

(25)   Which word is not like the other three?

   (A) compliant   (B) obstinate   (C) docile   (D) yielding

(26)   State the word in the brackets that is associated with the words in bold.

   Ice Hockey   [(A) chukker (B) jack (C) mallet (D) puck (E) cue]

(27)   State the word that rhymes with fete.

   (A) Betty   (B) skate   (C) feet   (D) Katy

(1)   State the correct meaning of the word MALICE.

     (A) TO JOIN ROPE   (B) EVIL   (C) A SMALL INSECT   (D) SPITE

(2)   State the number that comes next in the series? 3   4   8   9   18 ………

     (A) 17   (B) 19   (C) 21   (D) 23   (E) 25

(3)   Add 3 letters that make help then you have a word meaning <u>attack.</u>   *r*…………….…..

(4)   Add 3 letters that make a hearing organ and you have a <u>furry animal.</u>   *b*……………..

(5)   Add 3 letters that make a wild bird and then you have a <u>domestic bird.</u>   *f*………………

Write the missing colour.   (6) *The new car was slate* …………...

(7) *His paintings always had an azure* ………*background.* (8) *The room was pitch* ………… .

(9)   Judith sits in the middle of the classroom. The number of desks in each row is the same. She has two desks in front, behind and on either side of her. How many desks are there in the room?

     (A) 16   (B) 25   (D) 36   (D) 40   (E) 49

(10)   State the figure that comes next in sequence.

     (A)   (B)   (C)   (D)

(11)   Farmer Jones said, "*It rained more on Wednesday than Thursday, but there was more sunshine on Wednesday than Tuesday.*" Which of the three days was probably the wettest?

     (A) Tuesday   (B) Wednesday   (C) Thursday   (D) Insufficient information given.

The missing word must be made from all the letters of the word in bold.

(12)   *Mum will give me a list of groceries to buy for our camping weekend which I am sure **includes** a loaf of …………………… bread.*

(13)   What word does the middle letter of the abbreviation F.B.I. stand for? ………………………

(14)   State the word that is similar in meaning to the word ATTIRE.

   (A) CLOTHING   (B) RETREAT   (C) SHEETS   (D) TRIAL

Only one word of each pair is spelt correctly. State the correct one.

(15)   ocupy   occupy   (16) tobacco   tobbacco   (17) science   sciense

(18)   Rearrange these letters to form a continent: R F C A I A   ....

(19)   COLLECTION is to STAMPS as ANTHOLOGY is to ....

(20)   BUCK is to DOE as BOAR is to ....

Complete the word in each sentence by adding five letters.   These five letters make up a word.
Write the word again as an answer.

In a formal letter we use the word 're ....' instead of 'ask'.   (21) ....

The Leaning Tower of Pisa is being reinforced because it can possibly col....... (22) ....

*When designing a kitchen an architect should make sure there is adequate
bench and cup............. space.*   (23) ....

To make this sentence sensible, cross out one word and write one that rhymes with it.

The young lady has begun work as a lark in a government office in Canberra.   (24) ....

(25)   Which word is not like the other three?

   (A) courteous   (B) affable   (C) civil   (D) impertinent

(26)   State the word in brackets that is not associated with the word in bold.

   Shark   [(A) hammerhead   (B) thresher   (C) nurse   (D) barracuda   (E) whaler]

(27)   State the word that rhymes with the name Sean.

   (A) dawn   (B) sane   (C) keen   (D) ban

(1)   State the correct meaning of the word ADVERSARY.

       (A) A CELEBRATION   (B) DISTRESS
       (C) AN ENEMY OR OPPONENT   (D) UNFAVOURABLE

(2)   Write the number that comes next in the series? 2.5   7.5   4.5   9.5   6.5 ....

(3)   Add 4 letters that make a place to skate then you have a word meaning
      <u>take in water.</u>   *d*..................

(4)   Add 4 letters that make an arm or leg and you have a word
      meaning <u>ascend.</u>   *c* ....

(5)   Add 4 letters that make a fruit and then you have an ancient <u>weapon.</u>   *s* ....

Write the missing colour.   (6) *Her face was nut .... from being in the sun all week.*

(7) *The walls of the room were painted jade ....* (8) *Mum's jumper was shell ....*

(9)   The top floor of an office building was used for storage. There were no windows – only lighting. The owner decided to convert the floor to office space. He planned to place windows along one wall which was 28 metres long. If each window was to be 2 metres wide and 1 metre high and the space between windows or end walls had to be exactly 3 metres, how many windows did he order?

      3   4   5   6   7   8   9

(10)   State the figure that comes next in sequence.

      (A)   (B)   (C)   (D)

(11)   In an Olympic relay final, four nations competed. Australia came just behind the U.S.A. The U.S.A. was not first. Even the Australians were too fast for the Russians who were favoured to win the race. Write the order in which the nations finished. (The other nation was Germany).

                                      ....

The missing word must be made from all the letters of the word in bold.

(12) *It is advisable to bid with .... at any **auction** as it is easy to become carried away.*

(13)   What word does the first letter of the abbreviation R.S.L. stand for? ....

(14)   State the word that is similar in meaning to the word TIDINGS.

(A) NEWS   (B) LEFT-OVERS   (C) WAGES   (D) SONGS

Only one word of each pair is spelt correctly. State the correct one.

(15)   coppying   copying   (16) averadge   average   (17) noticeable   noticable

---

(18)   Rearrange these letters to form an ocean. C L T A N I A T   ....

---

(19)   SILO is to WHEAT as RESERVOIR is to ....

(20)   MASON is to STONE as GLAZIER is to ....

Complete the word in each sentence by adding five letters. These five letters make up a word.
Write the word again as an answer.

The armed forces in Australia are concerned with the de…….. of the country. (21) ....

A long period without any rain is known as a dr………….. .   (22) ....

Psychologists often ob ………. children's behaviour through a two-way mirror. (23) ....

To make this sentence sensible, cross out one word and write one that rhymes with it.

(24)   *To begin the meal we ordered a bowl of chicken stoop.*   (24) ....

---

(25)   Which word is not like the other three?

(A) genial   (B) touchy   (C) peevish   (D) testy

---

(26)   State the word in the brackets that is associated with the word in bold.

Cat   [(A) eland   (B) panther   (C) kudu   (D) impala   (E) gazelle]

---

(27)   State the word that rhymes with melee.

(A) sea   (B) play   (C) really   (D) jelly

---

(1)   State the correct meaning of the word IMPERATIVE.

(A) A ROYAL ORDER   (B) CANNOT BE PIERCED   (C) URGENT (D) NOT SORRY

(2)   Write the number that comes next in the series?   17   34   20   40   26   ......

(3)   Add 5 letters that make an old weapon then you have a word
meaning <u>look quickly.</u>   g.....................

(4)   Add 5 letters that make a narrow street and you have
<u>land between hills.</u>   v.....................

(5)   Add 5 letters that make a spherical shape and then you have
<u>some earth.</u>   g.....................

Write the word ending in 'ant'.   (6) *a person who rents a house from a landlord* t................

   (7) *a very large land animal* e...................   (8) *sweet smelling* f......................

(9)   In an enclosure at the zoo which housed some storks and hippopotamuses, Terry
counted 30 legs. There were exactly twice as many hippopotamuses as there were
storks. How many storks were there?

   1   2   3   4   5   6

(10)   State the figure that comes next in sequence.

   (A)   (B)   (C)   (D)

(11)   There were 13 cars held up at a red light. How many cars had an odd number of cars in
front and behind them? (The 13 cars were one behind the other).

   5   6   7   8   9

The missing word must be made from all the letters of the word in bold.

(12)   *The **Flemish** painter is famous for the portrait he did of* ....

(13)   Write the word with the prefix PAR that is <u>a light umbrella</u>.   ....

(14)   Write the word with the prefix PRO meaning <u>make longer in time</u>.   ....

(15)   Write the word with the prefix COM meaning <u>to pass on or transmit</u>.   ....

---

(16)   State the word that is similar in meaning to the word REMOTE.

   (A) VAST   (B) DISTANT   (C) EMPTY   (D) SMALL

Only one word of each pair is spelt correctly. State the correct one.

(17)   cieling   ceiling   (18) forfiet   forfeit   (19) comparing   compareing

---

(20)   Rearrange these letters to form a large river: Z N M A A O   ....

---

(21)   ORCHARD is to APPLES as VINEYARD is to ....

(22)   DONKEY is to BRAY as GOAT is to ....

Complete the word in each sentence by adding five letters. These five letters make up a word.
Write the word again as an answer.

The lowest rank in the police force is a cons................   (23)...................

If we put a photograph in an envelope with a letter we en.............. it.   (24) ....

At high school most students will study hi.............. .   (25) ....

To make this sentence sensible, cross out one word and write one that rhymes with it.

(26)   *The quantity of petrol purchased is measured in metres.*   ....

---

(27)   Which word is not like the other three?

   (A) blend   (B) amalgamate   (C) segregate   (D) mingle

---

(28)   State the word in the brackets that is not associated with the word in bold.

   Bee   [(A) drone   (B) queen   (C) wax   (D) hive   (E) termite]

---

(29)   State the word that rhymes with tirade. (A) lady   (B) stride   (C) blade   (D) scarred

---

(1)   State the correct meaning of the word BIZARRE.

(A) QUEER   (B) CROOKED
(C) SALE OF THINGS TO RAISE FUNDS   (D) ATTRACTIVE

(2)   Write the number that comes next in the series. 8800   880   88   8.8   ....

(3)   Add 5 letters that make a missile then you have a word meaning <u>not wide.</u>   *n*............

(4)   Add 5 letters that make a hostile feeling and you have a word meaning <u>peril.</u> *d*............

(5)   Add 5 letters to make 'less high' and you have <u>something grown in the garden.</u> *f*............

Write the word ending in 'ant'.

(6)   *a house or room that is empty is*   v.....................

(7)   *a person who buys and sells goods*   m.....................

(8)   *a hanging ornament such as a necklace or earring*   p.....................

(9)   The results of a mathematics test in our class placed Mary and Derek equal first. Then came Thomas and Rebecca who were equal third. Rebecca scored three marks less than Mary. If the combined marks of the four children was 330, what was Rebecca's score?

(A) 80   (B) 81   (C) 83   (D) 84   (E) 85

(10) State the figure on the right which is a mirror image (reversal) of the figure on the left of the vertical broken line shown.

(A)   (B)   (C)   (D)

(11) Trevor has four more toy cars than James and 2 more than Allen.
      Between the three boys they have 24 cars. How many has Allen?   ....

The missing word must be made from all the letters of the word in bold.

(12) *The motorist **blamed** the foggy weather for hitting a pedestrian who ....*
      across the road.

(13)   Write the word with the prefix PAR that is a place of extreme beauty – heaven.

....

(14)   State the word that is similar in meaning to the word CHIDE.

(A) FREEZE   (B) FRIGHTEN   (C) TEASE   (D) SCOLD

Only one word of each pair is spelt correctly . State the correct one.

(15)   column   collumn   (16) ornamant   ornament   (17) mystery   mistery

(18)   Rearrange these letters to form an Asian country: I D T A N H A L   ....

(19)   DRINK is to FIZZES as STEAM is to ....

(20)   JEW is to SYNAGOGUE as MUSLIM is to ....

Complete each simile by using the correct word.

(21) as .... as a hatter   (22) as .... as a doorpost

(23) as .... as a pikestaff   (24) as .... as an eel

(25) as .... as Methuselah   (26) as ....as a cricket

Write one word for several: (27)   a long deep wound or cut g...................

(28) a man who has never married b.................   (29)   burn with boiling water s..............

(30)   Which word is not like the other three?

(A) follower   (B) disciple   (C) leader   (D) supporter

(31)   State the word in the brackets that is associated with the word in bold.

Hospital [(A) dredge (B) theodolite (C) ammeter (D) barometer (E) thermometer]

(32)   State the word that rhymes with depot:

(A) trot   (B) despot   (C) flow   (D) report

(1)   State the correct meaning of the word PRECARIOUS.

       (A) VERY CAREFUL   (B) UNSAFE   (C) VALUABLE (D) VERY STEEP

(2)   Write the number that comes next in the series? $\dfrac{1}{2}$ $\dfrac{1}{4}$ $\dfrac{1}{8}$ $\dfrac{1}{16}$ ....

(3)   Add 5 letters that make an American word for farm and you have
     <u>part of a tree.</u>   b.................

(4)   Add 5 letters that make a group word for mountains and you have <u>a fruit.</u> o.................

(5)   Add 5 letters that make a form of transport and then you have a
     <u>word meaning to 'draw tight or stretch'.</u>   s.................

Write the word ending in 'ent'.   (6) *A person who is not guilty is* i.....................

(7)   *A person who has a good brain is* i.........................

(8)   *A person who is cheeky or rude is* i.........................

(9)   Dad goes shopping once a year for clothes. He bought an equal number of sports shirts
    at $18 and dress shirts for $25 at one department store. If he spent $215 altogether for
    these items, how many shirts did he buy altogether?

    5 6 7 8 9 10 11 12

(10)   State the figure on the right which is a mirror image (reversal of the figure on the left of
    the vertical broken line shown.

                                          (A)   (B)   (C)   (D)

(11)   Guy has 18 more marbles than Robert and 24 more than Steven. The three
    boys have 117 marbles between them. How many has Guy?   ....

The missing word must be made from all the letters of the word in bold.

(12)   *The actors spoke **German** in the nativity play and there was a real cow in the* ....

(13)   Write the word with the prefix PRO meaning to continue after stopping. ....

(14)   State the word that is similar in meaning to the word FALTER.

     (A) BRIDLE   (B) KNOT   (C) EXCHANGE   (D) HESITATE

Only one word of each pair is spelt correctly. State the correct one.

(15)   bussiness business   (16) illustrate ilustrate   (17) ellastic elastic

---

(18)   Rearrange these letters to form the fastest of the cat family. A T E H H E C ....

---

(19)   TOBACCO is to POUCH as GAS is to ....

(20)   BEE is to BUZZ as BEETLE is to ....

Complete each simile by using the correct word.

(21) *as .... as a peacock*   (22) *as ....as a feather*

(23) *as .... as Punch*   (24) *as .... as mustard*

(25) *as .... as the weather*   (26) *as .... as an ape*

Write one word for several.   (27) *a long sea journey v....................*

(28) *fragments of broken bricks or masonry r...............* (29) *a bad dream n....................*

---

(30)   Which word is not like the other three?

     (A) boisterous   (B) docile   (C) mild   (D) soft

---

(31)   State the word that is not associated with the other four words.

     (A) puree   (B) garnish   (C) seasoning   (D) etching   (E) sauce

---

(32)   State the word that rhymes with bouquet.

     (A) yet   (B) tray   (C) rat   (D) queue

---

(1)   State the correct meaning of the word SAVOUR.

(A) TASTE OR SMELL   (B) A RESCUER
(C) GOOD TO EAT   (D) A TYPE OF JACKET

(2)   Write the letters that come next in the series? a c d   d f g   g i j   j l m ....

Write two letters in the brackets that both end the first word and begin the next.

(3)   STAR (   ) NTILATOR   (4) POR (   ) ALLENGE (5) EAR (   ) ING

Write the word ending in 'ist' after each clue.

(6)   *a person who writes for a newspaper or magazine*   j................................

(7)   *a person who has studied plants*   b..............................

(8)   At school Elizabeth had a number of counters on her desk. She was moving them around and putting them into groups with equal numbers. When they were in groups of 2, 3 or 4 there was always one left over. If she put them in groups of 7 she found there were none left over. What is the least number of counters that she could have had on her desk?

7   21   35   49   56   63   70   77

(9)   State the figure on the right which is a mirror image (reversal) of the figure on the left of the vertical broken line.

(A)   (B)   (C)   (D)

(10)   Sandy is three times as old as Patty. In six years' time Sandy will be twice as old as Patty. How old is Patty now? ....

The missing word must be made from all the letters of the word in bold.

*(11)   When Mr Smith was called a '**damned**' liar, he was entitled to .... an apology.*

(12)   Write the word with the prefix TRANS meaning to change from one language to another.   ....

(13)   State the word that is similar in meaning to the word ADHERE.

(A) MEND   (B) ARRIVE   (C) REMOVE   (D) STICK

Only one word of each pair is spelt correctly. State the correct one.

(14)   procede   proceed   (15) fulfill   fulfil   (16) referred   refered

(17)   Rearrange these letters to form a sea creature with tentacles.
        S O O C U T P   ....

(18)   DEER is to STAG as DUCK is to ....

(19)   BIRDS are to AVIARY as FISH are to ....

Complete each simile by using the correct word.

(20)   as .... as crystal   (21) as .... as a bank

(22)   as .... as a dog   (23) as .... as dust

(24)   as .... as satin   (25) as .... as lead

Write one word for several. (26) *the decision of a jury*   v..................

(27) *a fully grown person* a........... (28) *a creature that gives milk to its young* m...............

(29)   Which word is not like the other three?

(A) burnished   (B) glazed   (C) tarnished   (D) polished

(30)   State the word that is not associated with the other four words.

(A) villa   (B) suburb   (C) cathedral   (D) bungalow   (E) palace

(31)   State the word that rhymes with gauge. (A) forge   (B) wage (C) seige (D) rouge

(32)   If A M W means B O X in code, what does B S O mean?   ....

(1)   State the correct meaning of the word PHYSIQUE.

(A) OF THE MIND   (B) A MEDICAL CURE
(C) THE BUILD AND SHAPE OF THE BODY   (D) MEDICINE

(2)   Write the letters that come next in the series? ac   ad   af   aj   ....

Write the letters in the brackets that both end the first word and begin the next.

(3)   EXH (   ) RALIA   (4) KING (   )INEER   (5) PRISO (   ) VOUS

Write the word ending in 'al' after each clue.

(6)   *something that is new or the first from which a copy is made*   o.........................

(7)   *relating to plants*   b.........................

(8)   *upright or plumb*   v.........................

(9)   During the course of an hour what is the difference in degrees through which the hour
       and the minute hands of a clock move?

       30   60   270   330   390   420

(10)   State the figure on the right which continues the sequence of three figures on the left.

       (A)   (B)   (C)   (D)

(11)   Mick is half as old as Jerry who is a teenager. In 14 years' time Mick will be
       three-quarters Jerry's age. How old is Jerry now?   ....

The missing word must be made from all the letters of the word in bold.

(12)   *His sneezing was **largely** due to an .... he had of pollen.*

(13)   Write the word with the prefix PER meaning 'forever'.   ....

(14)   State the word that is similar in meaning to the word CORPULENT.

   (A) FAT   (B) CHEEKY   (C) DISHONEST   (D) RUDE

Only one word of each pair is spelt correctly. State the correct one.

(15)   niece   neice   (16) frieght   freight   (17) agreable   agreeable

---

(18)   Rearrange these letters to form a state in Australia. T I C A I R O V ....

---

(19)   TELEPHONE is to RING as FIRE is to ....

(20)   OPTOMETRIST is to EYES as CHIROPODIST is to ....

The words below are written in shortened or abbreviated form. Write the full word alongside.

(21)   *flu* ....   (22)   *exam* ....

(23)   *plane* ....   (23)   *fridge* ....

(24)   *cello* ....   (25)   *bus* ....

Write one word for **several**:   (27)   *coat thickly with paint*   d........................

(28)   *fit to be eaten* e...................   (29)   *not natural or real*   a........................

---

(30)   Which word is not like the other three?

   (A) connect   (B) interlace   (C) unite   (D) separate

---

(31)   State the word that is not associated with the other four words.

   (A) fez   (B) sarong   (C) beret   (D) turban   (E) bowler

---

(32)   State the word that rhymes with obese. (A) chase (B) piece (C) sneeze (D) messy

---

(33)   If H M E means F O G in code, what does Q S R mean?   ....

---

(1) State the correct meaning of the word INSULATE.

(A) AMBUSH (B) COUNT
(C) RISE IN REVOLT (D) PROTECT FROM LOSS OF HEAT OR ELECTRICITY

(2) Write the letters that come next in the series? by cx dw ev ....

Write two letters in the brackets that both end the first word and begin the next.

(3) MUTT ( ) LY (4) GARA ( ) NEROUS (5) MIRR ( ) GAN

Write the word ending in 'ic' after each clue.

(6) *a word that means the opposite to 'private'* p.........................

(7) *a word that describes someone who loves his or her country.* p.........................

(8) *a car that changes gear by itself is* a.........................

(9) Trevor is three times as old as Janette. Two years ago Janette was twice as old as William. William is one fifth of Trevor's age. Who will be 11 next birthday?

(A) Trevor (B) Janette (C) William (D) Not enough information given

(10) State one of the figures that is odd or different from the other four.

(A) (B) (C) (D) (E)

(11) How many one-centimetre cubes can be packed in a rectangular box 6cm by 2 cm by 3 cm? ....,,,

The missing word must be made from all the letters of the word in bold.

(12) *Instruments for the doctor to perform the operation on the soldier's **duodenal** ulcer were*

.... from the helicopter.

(13) Write the word with the prefix SUPER meaning higher in position. ....

(14)   State the word that is similar in meaning to the word NEGOTIATE.

(A) EXPEL   (B) ATTEMPT   (C) REFUSE   (D) ARRANGE

Only one word of each pair is spelt correctly. State the correct one.

(15)   loveing   loving   (16) heifer   hiefer   (17) gorgious gorgeous

---

(18)   Rearrange these letters to form a capital city in Europe. D D I A M R   ....

---

(19)   HERD is to CATTLE as REGIMENT is to ....

(20)   DEPOT is to BUSES as HANGAR is to ....

In the list below cross out all the flowers and you are left with trees. Write the tree that has the most vowels.

geranium   gladioli   hickory   mahogany   dahlia   palm   phlox   acacia

(21)   ....

Write one word for several.   (22)   an extra payment   b.................

(23)   blind with brightness   d....................   (24)   give up entirely a........................

---

(25)   Which word is not like the other three?

(A) ridiculous   (B) idiotic   (C) rational   (D) absurd

---

(26)   State the word that is not associated with the other four words.

(A) culottes   (B) leotards   (C) blazers   (D) wellingtons   (E) tuxedos

---

(27)   State the word that rhymes with eyrie. (A) lyre   (B) cheery (C) diary (D) ferry

---

(28)   If the code word for COME is F R P H, what does V W R S mean? ....

(1)   State the correct meaning of the word HEREDITY.

(A) FRIENDLINESS   (B) RELATED
(C) QUALITIES COMING FROM PARENTS (D) KNOWLEDGE OF COATS OF ARMS

(2)   Which number is the odd one out in the group?

13   15   19   21   24   27   29   31

Write two letters in the brackets that both end the first word and begin the next.

(3)   WHI (   ) IPPING   (4)   WIND (   ) ASE   (5)   COA (   ) ERILE

Write the word ending in 'ate' after each clue.

(6)   *to think*   m..........................   (7)   *to copy*   d..........................

(8)   *to end*   t..........................   (9)   *to recover*   r..........................

(10)   *to look into*   i..........................   (11)   *to shorten*   a..........................

(12)   What are the chances of throwing at least 10 when rolling a pair of unbiased dice?

$\dfrac{1}{36}$ $\dfrac{2}{36}$ $\dfrac{3}{36}$ $\dfrac{4}{36}$ $\dfrac{5}{36}$ $\dfrac{6}{36}$

(13)   State one of the figures that is odd or different from the other four.

(A)   (B)   (C)   (D)   (E)

(14)   How many two-centimetre cubes can be packed in a
rectangular box 12 cm × 8 cm × 6 cm?   ....

The missing word must be made from all the letters of the word in bold.

(15)   *The eminent philosopher delivered an hour long .... in **Ontario.***

(16)   Write the word with the prefix SUB meaning a pedestrian tunnel.   ....

(17)   State the word that is similar in meaning to the word SOMBRE.

(A) GLOOMY   (B) ASLEEP   (C) ANGRY   (D) PLEASED

Only one word of each pair is spelt correctly. Circle the correct one.

(18)   argument   arguement   (19) spacious   spaceious   (20) nameing   naming

---

(21)   Rearrange these letters to form the world's highest mountain. T R E E S E V

....

---

(22)   A SCULPTOR is to STONE as a JOINER is to ....

(23)   STRING is to PEARLS as BUNTING is to ....

Which of these words *equine   lupine   porcine   bovine* mean

(24)   like a cow? ....   (25) like a horse? ....

Write one word for several: (26) *a solemn promise*   o...........................

(27)   *shining brightly* r........................   (28) *pull down a building*   d........................

---

(29)   Which word is not like the other three?

(A) continuing   (B) lasting   (C) fleeting   (D) enduring

---

(30)   State the word that is not associated with the other four words.

(A) forgery   (B) treason   (C) homicide   (D) obesity   (D) blackmail

---

(31)   State the word that rhymes with debut.

(A) hut   (B) few   (C) rabbit   (D) foot

---

(32)   Write the third largest in size starting from the smallest.

(A) quintet   (B) duet   (C) solo   (D) sextet

---

(1) State the correct meaning of the word OMINOUS.

(A) VERY LARGE (B) LEFT OUT (C) COMPLETE POWER (D) THREATENING

(2) Which number is the odd one out in the group?

96 56 24 66 32 72 16 88

Write two letters in the brackets that both end the first word and begin the next.

(3) BREA (   ) ANK   (4) REAS (   ) CE   (5) COA (   ) OICE

Write the numeral words using each clue.

(6) *ten athletic events*   d.....................   (7) *five-sided figure*   p.....................

(8) *someone 100 years old*   c..................   (9) *four musicians*   q.....................

(10) *eyeglass for one eye*   m....................   (11) *three copies*   t.....................

(12) On a page of a natural history book Jerry saw pictures of insects and spiders. He counted the legs of all these creatures and noticed that there were twice as many spiders' legs as insects' legs. How many creatures were there on the page?

2 3 4 5 6 7 8 9

(13) State one of the figures that is odd or different from the other four.

(A)   (B)   (C)   (D)   (E)

Name the solid after each clue.

(14) *It has 2 triangular faces and 3 rectangular faces.*   ....

(15) *It has one square face and four triangular faces.*   ....

The missing word must be made from all the letters of the word in bold.

(16) *Dad was excited in the hardware store as he saw a **gadget** ....at half price.*

(17)   State the word that is similar in meaning to the word WARY.

    (A) CARELESS   (B) TIRED   (C) CAUTIOUS   (D) CUNNING

Supply the second word to make a common pair of words.

(18)   *pins and* .... (19) *hue and* .... (20) *beck and* ....

(21)   Rearrange these letters for form a breed of dog used by police. N A A L I T S A

    ....

(22)   CATHOLIC is to PRIEST as JEW is to ....

(23)   BURGUNDY is to RED as MAHOGANY is to ....

Write the word that would fit into both spaces.

(24)   *As the cricket* .... *was dead the bowler had to* .... *the ball up.*

Write one word for several: (25) *a person who searches for minerals* p...............

(26)   *a person who eats human flesh* c................ (27) *put off till later*   p...............

(28)   Which word is not like the other three?

    (A) abundance   (B) scarcity   (C) lack   (D) shortage

(29)   State the word that is not associated with the other four words.

    (A) terminal   (B) tower   (C) supersonic   (D) tarmac (E) stadium

Change each noun into its masculine form:

(30)   *bride* .... (31) *belle* .... (32) *spinster* ....

State a word on the right that would be part of the group on the left.

(33)   orbit galaxy gravity (A) hamster (B) planet (C) broadcast (D) vandal (E) stadium

(1)   State the correct meaning of the word PREMATURE.

(A) SCENES FROM A COMING FILM   (B) FULLY GROWN
(C) PLAN BEFOREHAND   (D) TOO SOON

(2)   Each half of a domino has a blank or 1, 2, 3, 4, 5 or 6 dots. The lowest is a double blank
and the highest a double six. How many dominoes are there in a set?

26   27   28   29   30   31   32   33   34

Write the letters in the brackets that both end the first word and begin the next.

(3)   MINIS (   ) RIFY   (4) VEHI (   ) ANER   (5) CALEN (   ) ING

Write the numeral words after each clue.

(6)   *plane with a single wing*   m.......................   (7) *having two feet*   b.................

(8)   *set of 8 musical notes*   o.......................   (9) *period of 10 years* d...............

(10)   *a sword fight between 2 people* d................   (11) *spear with 3 prongs* t..............

(12)   Five cubes were stuck together in the form of a cross. The cubes were then dipped in
paint and then allowed to dry. After pulling the cubes apart, how many of their faces
would be painted?

(A) 20   (B) 22   (C) 24   (D) 26   (E) 28

(13)   Which one of the figures is odd or different from the other four?

(A)   (B)   (C)   (D)   (E)

Name the solid after each clue.

(14)   *It has 1 circular base, 1 circular edge, 2 faces and 1 vertex.*   ....

(15)   *It has a triangular base and 3 triangular faces .*   ....

The missing word must be made from all the letters of the word in bold.

*(16)   In Hong Kong, Mum selected a piece of pure **gabardine** for a skirt and she
.... with the shopkeeper for ten minutes before settling the price.*

(17)   State the word that is similar in meaning to the word FUTILE.

      (A) USELESS   (B) SOON   (C) RICH   (D) FRAIL

Supply the second word to make a common pair of words.

(18)   *cut and* ....   (19) *rack and* ....   (20) *do or* ....

(21)   Rearrange these letters for form the world's largest mammal. E W L A H ....

(22)   JOHN BULL is to ENGLAND as UNCLE .... is to the U.S.A.

(23)   AUSTRALIA is to DOLLAR as JAPAN is to ....

Write the word that would fit into both spaces.

(24)   *Carrying a sawn-off* .... *the bandit leapt over the counter to* .... *the till.*

Write one word for several;   (25) *a river of ice*   g.................

(26) *a person who wears no clothes*   n............   (27) *shed fur or feathers* m..................

(28)   Which word in not like the other three?

      (A) primitive   (B) elementary   (C) primeval   (D) progressive

(29)   State the word that is not associated with the other five words.

      (A) plump   (B) pale   (C) spiteful   (D) freckled   (E) tall   (F) short

Change each noun into its masculine form.

(30)   *squaw* ....   (31) *lass* ....   (32) *duchess* ....

State the word on the right that would be part of the group on the left.

(33)   cheese cream milk (A) pickles (B) chutney (C) mayonnaise (D) yoghurt

(1)   State the correct meaning of the word OPAQUE.

      (A) NOT TRANSPARENT   (B) HAVING MANY COLOURS
      (C) WIDE OPEN   (D) NOT BELIEVING IN GOD

(2)   Malcolm Muscles, the champion axeman can cut through a tree trunk in 3 minutes.
If he was presented with one long log of equal thickness, how many minutes
would it take Malcolm to cut it into 10 equal pieces?   ....

Write the word that begins with the prefix 'en'.   (3)   *to join the armed forces* ....

(4)   *to put your name on a list* ....   (5)   *to cut letters on a hard surface* ....

State the object that you could eat in each group.

(6)   *trilby rasp doily strudel sedan*   (7)   *coracle angora yaw atoll caviar*

(8)   A wealthy sheik in the Middle East decided to give paper weights to his friends. Each
weight was a cube made of lead but coated with 2 mm of pure gold. To his male friends
he gave cubes that had 4 cm sides. The cubes he gave to his female friends had 1 cm
sides. What fraction in gold are the smaller cubes of the larger cubes?

$$\frac{1}{16} \quad \frac{1}{4} \quad \frac{1}{8} \quad \frac{1}{2} \quad \frac{1}{32}$$

(9)   Which one of the figures is odd or different from the other four?

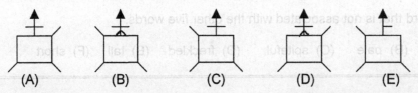

     (A)   (B)   (C)   (D)   (E)

Name the solid after each clue.

(10)   *It has 6 square faces.*   ....

(11)   *It has no edges or vertices and a surface that is always equidistant*
      from the centre.   ....

The missing word must be made from all the letters of the word in bold.

(12)   *The pest controller **certified** that he had .... the white ant problem in the*
building.

(13)   State the word that is similar in meaning to the word INTRIGUE.

(A) COMPLICATED   (B) PLOT   (C) ENQUIRE   (D) TRICK

Supply the second word to make a common pair of words.

(14)   *give and* ....   (15) *hale and* ....   (16) *hammer and* ....

(17)   Rearrange these letters to form a cold ocean. T T C I A C R N A   ....

Read each group of four words. Three have the same vowel sound. State the one that is different.

(18)   *bomb   plume   broom   tomb* ....

(19)   *cove   mauve   love   stove* ....

Write the word that would fit into both spaces.

(20)   *Last week a burglar* .... *my aunt's television and this week he came back for*

        her fur ....

Write one word for several: (21) *replace by a machine*   m....................

(22)   *roof of the mouth* p....................   (23) *people in church*   c........................

(24)   Which word is not like the other three?

(A) hinder   (B) obstruct   (C) tolerate   (D) prevent

(25)   State the word that is not associated with the other four words.

(A) pelican   (B) crane   (C) emu   (D) stork   (E) swan

Change each noun into its feminine form.

(26)   count ....   (27) nephew ....   (28) lord ....

(1)   State the correct meaning of the word IMPEDE.

    (A) SEND AWAY   (B) WALK ON FOOT   (C) HINDER   (D) ABOUT TO HAPPEN

Wayne has just moved into a new house. The width of the land on which it is built is 22m. He and his father are planning to erect a post and rail fence. They are going to use posts 2 metres apart and 3 rails to join each pair of posts. They want to build the first stage of the fence across the front this weekend.

(2)   How many posts must they order? ......   (3)   How many rails must they order? ......

Write the word that end with 'port'.   (4) *send goods overseas* ....

(5) *an account of something* ....   (6) *carry from one place to another* ....

State the correct answer in the brackets.

(7)   The word 'pizza' is pronounced: [(A) pitzer   (B) peetzer   (C) pyser   (D) piecer]

---

(8)   Out of 100 planes on an aircraft carrier there were 20 more twin-engined jets than those with single engines. One in ten of the twin-engined jets carried surveillance equipment and cameras with no weapons aboard. What percentage of the aircraft on the ship carried weapons?

    (A) 80   (B) 86   (C) 90   (D) 92   (E) 94

---

(9)   Which one of the figures is odd or different from the other four?

    (A)   (B)   (C)   (D)   (E)

---

(10)   Geoff has 2 more coloured pencils than Trevor and 6 less than Vince. If all three boys have 16 coloured pencils between them, how many has Vince?   ....

The missing word must be made from all the letters of the word in bold.

(11)   *My brother is studying zoology at the university and my father posted a* **manilla** *envelope to him containing a book on* .... *behaviour.*

---

(12)   What does the third letter of the abbreviation Y.W.C.A. stand for? ....

---

(13) State the word that is similar in meaning to the word ENCOUNTER.

(A) CALCULATOR   (B) MEETING   (C) STORY   (D) ACCIDENT

Supply the word, which is a food, to each idiom.

(14) *bring home the* ....   (15) .... *of one's eye.*

---

(16) Rearrange these letters to form an intelligent ape. E A Z E P H C I N M ....

Read each group of four words. Three have the same vowel sound. State the one that is different.

(17) caught   nought   draught   fort   ....

(18) world   spawn   born   caulk   ....

Write the word that would fit into both spaces.

(19) *If Duncan can* .... *the form he showed in his last tennis* .... *then he will win easily.*

Write one word for several: (20) *import or export goods secretly* s...............

(21) *plant or animal that feeds on another* p............... (22) *free in giving* g.................

---

(23) Which word is not like the other three?

(A) insipid   (B) savoury   (C) tasty   (D) appetising

---

(24) State the word that is not associated with the other four words.

(A) hazy   (B) squally   (C) sultry   (D) chubby   (E) misty

The American form of the word is given. Write the English or Australian form next to each one.

(25) *gasoline* .... (26) *faucet* .... (27) *streetcar* ....

State the correct answer.

(28) *A psychologist understands: (A) food (B) poisons (C) insects (D) plants (E) behaviour*

---

(1)   State the correct meaning of the word SAGACIOUS.

(A) READY TO ATTACK   (B) GREEDY   (C) SINKING DOWN   (D) WISE

(2)   If the Romans played cricket and a batsman made a record CCCXXVI,
how many runs was this?   ....

Write each word that has a 'ph' sound.   (3) *a game bird in Europe* ....

(4) *a group of words that is not a sentence*..............   (5) *a small glass bottle* ....

(6) *a young person whose mother and father are dead* ....

State the correct answer in the brackets.

(7)   The word 'route' rhymes with: [(A) shoot   (B) doughty   (C) shout   (D) riot]

(8)   Mum gave Josephine money to buy a quantity of mangoes, melons and passion fruit at
the greengrocer's. The melons were $4 each, the mangoes $1 each and the passion
fruit were 50c each. Josephine spent $19 and brought 20 pieces of fruit home. It she
bought twice as many mangoes as melons, how many passion fruit did she bring home?

2   4   6   8   10   12   14   16

(9)   Which one of the figures is odd or different from the other four?

(A)   (B)   (C)   (D)   (E)

(10)   A professional golfer takes 3 different pairs of pants, 4 sweaters and 2 pairs of shoes to
a tournament. In how many different ways can he dress himself?

(A) 9   (B) 14   (C) 11   (D) 24

The missing word must be made from all the letters of the word in bold.

(11)   *It was **shattering** news for my father who had to pay $5000 for the dentist to* ....
my front teeth.

(12)   What does the fourth letter of the abbreviation R.S.P.C.A. stand for? ....

(13)   State the word that is similar in meaning to the word HUMID.

   (A) FURIOUS   (B) HAPPY   (C) MOIST   (D) FUNNY

Supply the word, which is a food, to each idiom.

(14)   *finger in every* ....   (15) *a piece of* .... *(easy).*

(16)   Rearrange these letters to form the tallest animal. F E F A I G R   ....

Read each group of four words. Three have the same vowel sound. State the one that is different.

(17)   mouth   moult   clout   south ....(18)   worth   worry   hurt   girth...............

Write the word that would fit into both spaces:

(19)   *The dog has a* .... *of young puppies so do not drop any* .... *around.*

Write one word for: (20)   *extremely ugly h* ....

(21)   *light rain d*...................   (22)   *hard-working   i*.........................

(23)   Which word is not like the other three?

   (A) strife   (B) combat   (C) harmony   (D) conflict

(24)   State the word that is not associated with the other three words.

   (A) bayonet   (B) grenade   (C) fuselage   (D) mortar

The American form of the word is given. Write the English or Australian form next to each one.

(25)   *railroad* ....   (26)   *sidewalk* ....   (27) *ketchup* ....

State the correct answer.

(28)   *A gourmet understands about:*

   (A) *sailing*   (B) *housing*   (C) *shooting*   (D) *cooking*   (E) *dancing*

(1)   State the correct meaning of the word SIMULATE.

   (A) AT THE SAME TIME   (B) MAKE A PRETENCE OR LIKENESS
   (C) SHAKE   (D) SORT OUT

John's teacher wrote the year of his birth on the board in the Roman numerals MCMLXV.

(2)   In what year was the teacher born? ....   (3) What century was this? ....

Write each word that ends in 'logue'.   (4) *a conversation* ....

(5)   *a speech by one person* ....   (6) *a list or record* ....

State the correct answer in the brackets.

(7)   The word 'suite' rhymes with: [(A) flute   (B) fleet   (C) suet   (D) sight]

(8)   A combined camp stove and heater run off two portable gas tanks. One tank will run for
       12 hours and the other for 8 hours before running out of gas. If both tanks are full and
       then turned on, after how many hours will there be twice as much gas in one tank as the
       other?   *(Hint: Use trial and error: try 2h, 4h .... in turn.*
                       Thus in 2h, first tank uses 2/12 = 1/6 of gas. Second tank uses 2/8 = ¼ gas.
                       But ¼ is not double 1/6 and hence 2h is not correct. Now try 4h and so on).

       2   4   6   8   10   12

(9)   Solve the relationship between the figures.

       ⌐ is to └ as ╱ is to   7   √   ╲   7
                              (A) (B) (C) (D)

(10)   A 70m long jet airliner has 3 classes of travel – first, business and economy.
       It uses 1/7 of its length for first class and the cockpit. What fraction of the
       fuselage is taken up by economy class if business class takes up 20m? ....

The missing word must be made from all the letters of the word in bold.

(11)   *The owner of the business was **feeling** very upset when he saw the bandit ....*
       with his week's takings.

(12)   What does the second capital letter of the abbreviation C.of E. stand for?....................

(13)   If the perimeter of a square is 64 cm, what is its area is square centimetres? ....

(14)   State the word that is similar in meaning to the word THEME.

    (A) NOVEL   (B) TOPIC   (C) CHAPTER   (D) PARAGRAPH

Supply the word, which is a creature, to each idiom.

(15)   *stir up a .... nest*   (16) *packed like ....*

(17)   Rearrange these letters to form the capital of the U.S.A. T N H A W N O I G S

    ....

Read each group of four words. Three have the same vowel sound. Write the one that is different.

(18)   halt fault gaunt salt ....   (19) chewed feud lewd   gourd ....

Write the word that would fit into both spaces:

(20)   *Marcia drew her .... around her as the ship approached the .... of Good Hope.*

Write one word for: (21)   *that is able to be seen v......................*

(22)   *happening at the same time s.........................*   (23) *to sleep lightly d..................*

(24)   Which word is not like the other three?

    (A) proffer   (B) donate   (C) supply   (D) retain

(25)   State the word that is not associated with the other four words.

    (A) clipper   (B) chariot   (C) sampan (D) gondola (E) punt

Write the secondary colour obtained by mixing the two primary colours.

(26)   *Blue plus yellow makes ....*   (27)   *Red plus yellow makes ....*

State the correct answer.

(28)   *An academic is likely to be interested in:*

    (A) sailing   (B) housing   (C) shooting   (D) cooking   (E) studying

(1)   State the correct meaning of the word COPIOUS.

   (A) NEAT   (B) SUCCESSFUL   (C) CAREFUL   (D) PLENTIFUL

(2)   State the right-angled triangle.

            (A)   (B)   (C)   (D)

Write each word that ends in 'ine'.   (3)   *to look closely at   e.......................*

(4)   *a type of small drum t................*   (5)   *a weekly or monthly publication m.................*

State the correct answer in the brackets.

(6)   The word 'yoga' rhymes with: [(A) ogre   (B) jogger   (C) brogue   (D) logo]

(7)   Whilst studying for a general aptitude test Brian attempted three practice papers. Brian
        scored 18 right the first time and 24 right the second. If he improves **at the same rate**,
        what will he score in the next practice test?

        30   31   32   33   34   35   36

(8)   Solve the relationship between the figures.

        ⟩ is to ◇◇ as ⟩ is to   8   ∞   ∽   ∞
                                     (A)   (B)   (C)   (D)

(9)   Inside the foyer of a modern hotel was a rectangular fish pond which measured 7 metres
        by 4 metres.   Around the edge was a border of golden coloured tiles 1 metre wide.
        How many square metres of this tiling was around the pond?
        ....

The missing word must be made from all the letters of the word in bold.

(10)   *The **licensed** publican .... to serve people who enter his hotel without shoes.*

(11)   What does the third letter of the abbreviation R.I.P. stand for?   ....

(12) Next year Tom's age will be a square number. Seven years ago his age was a cube number. How old is Tom now? ....

(13) State the word that is similar in meaning to the word PRUDENT.

(A) STUPID   (B) CHEEKY   (C) WISE   (D) STRONG

Supply the word, which is a creature, to each idiom.

(14) *shed* .... *tears*   (15)   *put the cart before the* ....

(16) Rearrange these letters for form Australia's greatest cricketer. M N B D R A A

....

Read each group of four words. Three have the same vowel sound. Write the one that is different.

(17) gait heap crepe tape .... (18) joke caulk yolk stoke ....

Write the word that would fit into both spaces.

(19)   *On the* .... *the fish weighed 10.4 kilograms but weighed 1.7 kilograms less when we scraped off the* .... *and took out the innards.*

Write one word for: (20) *causing death or disaster*   f..................

(21) *desire for success*   a..................   (22) *feathers of a bird*   p.......................

(23) Which word is not like the other three?

(A) savage   (B) barbarous   (C) humane   (D) pitiless

(24) State the acronym that is associated with the landing on the moon.

(A) UNICEF   (B) ANZAC   (C) NATO   (D) NASA

(25) State the word that is not associated with the other three.

(A) quotient   (B) dividend   (C) product   (D) distil

State the correct answer.

(26)   *A mercenary is likely to be interested in:*

(A) *fighting*   (B) *shooting*   (C) *cooking*   (D) *studying singing*

Choose answers from the list above each series of questions.

WRITERS: Dickens   Barrie   Grahame   Kipling   Tolkien   Twain   Milne   Carroll   Verne

Who wrote:

(1) Just So Stories ....

(2) 20 000 Leagues Under the Sea.......................

(3) The Adventures of Tom Sawyer ....

(4) Alice's Adventures in Wonderland ....

(5) The Wind in the Willows...........................

(6) The Hobbit ....   (7) Peter Pan..............

(8) When We Were Very Young.......................

(9) David Copperfield

DOCTORS: Jenner   Salk   Lister   Fleming   Mesmer   Barnard   Roentgen   Laennec

(10) Performed first heart transplant................

(11) Invented the stethoscope..............................

(12) Developed antiseptics ....

(13) First to innoculate against smallpox ....

(14) Discovered a polio vaccine ....

(15) Discovered penicillin ....

(16) Discovered x-rays ....

(17) First used hypnotism in medicine ....

FAMOUS PEOPLE: Tutankhamen   Rommel   Wright   Magellan   Marx

Hitler   Cleopatra   Fawkes   Einstein   Hannibal   Daimler   Caesar   Bell   Napoleon

Drake   Melba   Galileo   Pavlova   Nightingale   Montezuma   Parkes   Ghandi

(18) Founder of Communism.........................

(19) Roman general who invaded Britain.............

(20) German-American physicist.....................

(21) Carthaginian general ....

(22) Early Australian statesman......................

(23) Early German car maker.........................

(24) Russian ballerina..................................

(25) Flew the first powered plane....................

(26) German field marshall............................

(27) Pioneered nursing ....

(28) Boy king of Egypt ....

(29) Last Aztec emperor of Mexico ....

(30) American inventor of telephone ....

(31) French Emperor....................................

(32) Portuguese navigator ....

(33) Italian astronomer.................................

(34) German dictator ....

(35) Hindu nationalist & spiritual leader ....

(36) English conspirator................................

(37) Queen of Egypt....................................

(38) Australian soprano ....

(39) English sailor ....

PAPER 1 **(1)** GLOWING AND FIERY **(2)** 17 **(3)** heart **(4)** Manchester **(5)** (C) **(6)** 8 **(7)** ANTLER **(8)** gas **(9)** brother's daughter **(10)** DISASTER **(11)** entrance **(12)** archery **(13)** audible **(14)** W **(15)** $10 **(16)** fit **(17)** use **(18)** end **(19)** CHEESE **(20)** plum **(21)** banana **(22)** pomegranate **(23)** material

PAPER 2 **(1)** A SMALL ALLOWANCE OF MONEY **(2)** 48 **(3)** eye **(4)** 13 **(5)** (D) **(6)** $19.05 **(7)** RIFLES **(8)** FRIENDLY **(9)** soles **(10)** BUILDING **(11)** doctor **(12)** fragrant **(13)** gorgeous **(14)** RED **(15)** 34 **(16)** son **(17)** are **(18)** ice **(19)** ROBBER **(20)** salmon **(21)** flathead **(22)** finch **(23)** stone

PAPER 3 **(1)** HOARSE OR HARSH SOUNDING **(2)** 23 **(3)** yellow **(4)** 1 **(5)** (C) **(6)** 6 **(7)** GRENADE **(8)** QUARRY **(9)** stationery **(10)** principal **(11)** REBUKE **(12)** bicycle **(13)** disappear **(14)** propeller **(15)** A E F H I **(16)** Judy **(17)** own **(18)** age **(19)** ate **(20)** glade **(21)** goat **(22)** sow **(23)** lynx **(24)** gem

PAPER 4 **(1)** A MISTAKEN IDEA **(2)** 1.1 **(3)** sleep **(4)** Sam **(5)** (C) **(6)** 7 **(7)** tablet **(8)** CUTLERY **(9)** dessert **(10)** JURISDICTION **(11)** occurred **(12)** movable **(13)** government **(14)** M **(15)** back **(16)** hen **(17)** ant **(18)** ate **(19)** zone **(20)** carrot **(21)** potato **(22)** undulating **(23)** mislay

PAPER 5 **(1)** VERY DEEP **(2)** 0.075 **(3)** dyspepsia **(4)** James **(5)** (B) **(6)** 0 **(7)** danger **(8)** hat or hats **(9)** gorilla **(10)** sheer **(11)** MILD **(12)** skilful **(13)** parallel **(14)** possess **(15)** S **(16)** south west **(17)** did **(18)** led **(19)** ten **(20)** crow **(21)** lion **(22)** jaguar **(23)** nitrogen **(24)** cereal

PAPER 6 **(1)** WILDLY EXCITED OR FEVERISH **(2)** 0.15 **(3)** straw **(4)** words **(5)** eggs **(6)** (A) **(7)** (C) **(8)** 15 **(9)** palest **(10)** MONK **(11)** storeys **(12)** ore **(13)** SHOWY **(14)** guard **(15)** handkerchief **(16)** immediately **(17)** 2 **(18)** south east **(19)** ass **(20)** ale **(21)** age **(22)** mole **(23)** snake **(24)** (C) **(25)** mineral

PAPER 7 **(1)** MAKE SIGNS WITH THE HANDS **(2)** (B) **(3)** speech **(4)** bites **(5)** moss **(6)** cat **(7)** Marcia **(8)** (B) **(9)** 12 **(10)** sauce **(11)** BEGINNING **(12)** woollen **(13)** buried **(14)** beautiful **(15)** 0 **(16)** ROSE **(17)** GOAT **(18)** the **(19)** lay **(20)** act **(21)** zoomed **(22)** Victoria **(23)** Danube **(24)** quay

PAPER 8 **(1)** GIVE WHEN ONE DIES **(2)** $\frac{9}{10}$ **(3)** ears **(4)** boils **(5)** choosers **(6)** lining **(7)** Martin **(8)** (D) **(9)** 6 **(10)** adders **(11)** BEG **(12)** rhythm **(13)** address **(14)** bilious **(15)** D E F **(16)** ROBIN **(17)** ANT **(18)** stem **(19)** ease **(20)** hood **(21)** jive **(22)** Eyre **(23)** novel **(24)** weighed

PAPER 9 **(1)** GREATNESS AND SPLENDOUR **(2)** G **(3)** breathing **(4)** nine **(5)** lost **(6)** leap **(7)** (D) **(8)** (C) **(9)** (A) **(10)** aisle **(11)** Flying **(12)** SLOW **(13)** February **(14)** cemetery **(15)** Wednesday **(16)** 4 **(17)** GNAT **(18)** OPAL **(19)** rage **(20)** pose **(21)** band **(22)** zealous **(23)** admiral **(24)** bungling **(25)** tree

PAPER 10 **(1)** A SPLIT OR CRACK **(2)** 16 **(3)** foot **(4)** shy **(5)** hot **(6)** child **(7)** 5 **(8)** (C) **(9)** Wednesday **(10)** finger **(11)** Royal **(12)** DOUBTFUL **(13)** umbrella **(14)** unconscious **(15)** forty **(16)** October **(17)** TRUMPET **(18)** REFINERY **(19)** time **(20)** vent **(21)** test **(22)** queue **(23)** (D) **(24)** affluent **(25)** card

PAPER 11 **(1)** SEEMING TO BE TRUE **(2)** 129 **(3)** sugar **(4)** green **(5)** rose **(6)** pink **(7)** $60 **(8)** (D) **(9)** Mizda, 3rd **(10)** mango **(11)** Australian **(12)** SACRED **(13)** grammar **(14)** jeweller **(15)** sugar **(16)** 9 **(17)** LEATHER **(18)** GANDER **(19)** form **(20)** pose **(21)** sage **(22)** scene **(23)** cello **(24)** harshness **(25)** froth

PAPER 12 **(1)** LOSE COURAGE OR HOPE **(2)** 21 **(3)** pink **(4)** pass **(5)** mate **(6)** yellow **(7)** green **(8)** black **(9)** 9 **(10)** (A) **(11)** John **(12)** cheat **(13)** Petroleum **(14)** calm **(15)** irritable **(16)** supervisor **(17)** oblige **(18)** I **(19)** FURNITURE **(20)** BANANAS **(21)** fare **(22)** face **(23)** keys **(24)** treasure **(25)** florid **(26)** discs **(27)** spite

PAPER 13 **(1)** KEENNESS AND ZEAL **(2)** 0.75 **(3)** kill **(4)** mask **(5)** lash **(6)** red **(7)** green **(8)** blue **(9)** 12 **(10)** (A) **(11)** F **(12)** secure **(13)** Hill **(14)** balanced **(15)** occasion **(16)** separate **(17)** enrol **(18)** LMNOP **(19)** CREAK **(20)** SCABBARD **(21)** rate **(22)** able **(23)** dish **(24)** youth **(25)** obstinate **(26)** puck **(27)** skate

PAPER 14 **(1)** SPITE **(2)** 19 **(3)** raid **(4)** bear **(5)** fowl **(6)** grey **(7)** blue **(8)** black **(9)** 25 **(10)** (A) **(11)** Tuesday **(12)** unsliced **(13)** Bureau **(14)** CLOTHING **(15)** occupy **(16)** tobacco **(17)** science **(18)** AFRICA **(19)** POEMS or STORIES **(20)** SOW **(21)** quest **(22)** lapse **(23)** board **(24)** clerk **(25)** impertinent **(26)** barracuda **(27)** dawn

PAPER 15 **(1)** AN ENEMY OR OPPONENT **(2)** 11.5 **(3)** drink **(4)** climb **(5)** spear **(6)** brown **(7)** green **(8)** pink **(9)** 5 **(10)** (D) **(11)** Germany, U.S.A., Australia, Russia **(12)** caution **(13)** Returned **(14)** NEWS **(15)** copying **(16)** average **(17)** noticeable **(18)** ATLANTIC **(19)** WATER **(20)** GLASS **(21)** fence **(22)** ought **(23)** serve **(24)** soup **(25)** genial **(26)** panther **(27)** play

PAPER 16 **(1)** URGENT **(2)** 52 **(3)** glance **(4)** valley **(5)** ground **(6)** tenant **(7)** elephant **(8)** fragrant **(9)** 3 **(10)** (B) **(11)** 6 **(12)** himself **(13)** PARASOL **(14)** PROLONG **(15)** COMMUNICATE **(16)** DISTANT **(17)** ceiling **(18)** forfeit **(19)** comparing **(20)** AMAZON **(21)** GRAPES **(22)** BLEAT **(23)** table **(24)** close **(25)** story **(26)** litres **(27)** segregate **(28)** termite **(29)** blade

ANSWERS

PAPER 17 **(1)** QUEER **(2)** 0.88 **(3)** narrow **(4)** danger **(5)** flower **(6)** vacant **(7)** merchant **(8)** pendant **(9)** 81 **(10)** (D) **(11)** 8 **(12)** ambled **(13)** PARADISE **(14)** scold **(15)** column **(16)** ornament **(17)** mystery **(18)** THAILAND **(19)** HISSES **(20)** MOSQUE **(21)** mad **(22)** deaf **(23)** plain **(24)** slippery **(25)** old **(26)** lively **(27)** gash **(28)** bachelor **(29)** scald **(30)** leader **(31)** thermometer **(32)** flow

---

PAPER 18 **(1)** UNSAFE **(2)** $\frac{1}{32}$ **(3)** branch **(4)** orange **(5)** strain **(6)** innocent **(7)** intelligent **(8)** impertinent, impudent **(9)** 10 **(10)** (B) **(11)** 53 **(12)** manger **(13)** PROCEED **(14)** hesitate **(15)** business **(16)** illustrate **(17)** elastic **(18)** CHEETAH **(19)** CYLINDER **(20)** DRONE **(21)** proud **(22)** light **(23)** pleased **(24)** keen **(25)** changeable, fickle **(26)** hairy **(27)** voyage **(28)** rubble **(29)** nightmare **(30)** boisterous **(31)** etching **(32)** tray

---

PAPER 19 **(1)** TASTE OR SMELL **(2)** m o p **(3)** VE **(4)** CH **(5)** LY, TH **(6)** journalist **(7)** botanist **(8)** 49 **(9)** (A) **(10)** 6 **(11)** demand **(12)** translate **(13)** STICK **(14)** proceed **(15)** fulfil **(16)** referred **(17)** OCTOPUS **(18)** DRAKE **(19)** AQUARIUM **(20)** clear **(21)** safe **(22)** sick **(23)** dry **(24)** smooth **(25)** heavy **(26)** verdict **(27)** adult **(28)** mammal **(29)** tarnished **(30)** suburb **(31)** wage **(32)** CUP

PAPER 20 **(1)** THE BUILD AND SHAPE OF THE BODY **(2)** a r **(3)** AUST **(4)** DOM **(5)** NER **(6)** original **(7)** botanical **(8)** vertical **(9)** 330 **(10)** (A) **(11)** 14 **(12)** allergy **(13)** PERMANENT **(14)** FAT **(15)** niece **(16)** freight **(17)** agreeable **(18)** VICTORIA **(19)** CRACKLE **(20)** FEET **(21)** influenza **(22)** examination **(23)** aeroplane **(24)** refrigerator **(25)** violoncello **(26)** omnibus **(27)** daub **(28)** edible **(29)** artificial **(30)** separate **(31)** sarong **(32)** piece **(33)** OUT

PAPER 21 **(1)** PROTECT FROM LOSS OF HEAT OR ELECTRICITY **(2)** fu **(3)** ON **(4)** GE **(5)** OR **(6)** public **(7)** patriotic **(8)** automatic **(9)** Janette **(10)** (C) **(11)** 36 **(12)** unloaded **(13)** SUPERIOR **(14)** arrange **(15)** loving **(16)** heifer **(17)** gorgeous **(18)** MADRID **(19)** SOLDIERS **(20)** AEROPLANES, PLANES **(21)** acacia **(22)** bonus **(23)** dazzled **(24)** abandon **(25)** rational **(26)** wellingtons **(27)** cheery **(28)** STOP

PAPER 22 **(1)** QUALITIES COMING FROM PARENTS **(2)** 24 **(3)** CH, SK **(4)** ER **(5)** ST **(6)** meditate **(7)** duplicate **(8)** terminate **(9)** recuperate **(10)** investigate **(11)** abbreviate **(12)** $\frac{6}{36}$ **(13)** (c) **(14)** 72 **(15)** oration **(16)** SUBWAY **(17)** gloomy **(18)** argument **(19)** spacious **(20)** naming **(21)** EVEREST **(22)** WOOD **(23)** FLAGS **(24)** bovine **(25)** equine **(26)** oath **(27)** radiant **(28)** demolish **(29)** fleeting **(30)** obesity **(31)** few **(32)** quintet

---

PAPER 23 **(1)** THREATENING **(2)** 66 **(3)** TH **(4)** ON **(5)** CH **(6)** decathlon **(7)** pentagon **(8)** centenarian **(9)** quartet **(10)** monocle **(11)** triplicates **(12)** 5 **(13)** (D) **(14)** triangular prism **(15)** square pyramid **(16)** tagged **(17)** CAUTIOUS **(18)** needles **(19)** cry **(20)** call **(21)** ALSATIAN **(22)** RABBI **(23)** BROWN **(24)** pitch **(25)** prospector **(26)** cannibal **(27)** postpone **(28)** abundance **(29)** stadium **(30)** bridegroom, groom **(31)** beau **(32)** bachelor **(33)** planet

---

ANSWERS

PAPER 24 **(1)** TOO SOON **(2)** 28 **(3)** TER **(4)** CLE **(5)** DAR **(6)** monoplane **(7)** biped **(8)** octave **(9)** decade **(10)** duel **(11)** trident **(12)** 22 **(13)** (E) **(14)** cone **(15)** triangular pyramid **(16)** bargained **(17)** USELESS **(18)** dried **(19)** ruin **(20)** die **(21)** WHALE **(22)** SAM **(23)** YEN **(24)** rifle **(25)** glacier **(26)** nudist **(27)** moult **(28)** progressive **(29)** spiteful **(30)** brave **(31)** lad **(32)** duke **(33)** yoghurt

---

PAPER 25 **(1)** NOT TRANSPARENT **(2)** 27 **(3)** enlist **(4)** enrol **(5)** engrave **(6)** strudel **(7)** caviar **(8)** $\frac{1}{16}$ **(9)** (E) **(10)** cube **(11)** sphere **(12)** rectified **(13)** PLOT **(14)** take **(15)** hearty **(16)** tongs **(17)** ANTARCTIC **(18)** bomb **(19)** love **(20)** stole **(21)** mechanise **(22)** palate **(23)** congregation **(24)** tolerate **(25)** emu **(26)** countess **(27)** niece **(28)** lady

---

PAPER 26 **(1)** HINDER **(2)** 12 **(3)** 33 **(4)** export **(5)** report **(6)** transport **(7)** peetzer **(8)** 94 **(9)** (B) **(10)** 10 **(11)** animal **(12)** Christian **(13)** MEETING **(14)** bacon **(15)** apple **(16)** CHIMPANZEE **(17)** draught **(18)** world **(19)** match **(20)** smuggle **(21)** parasite **(22)** generous **(23)** insipid **(24)** chubby **(25)** petrol **(26)** tap **(27)** tram **(28)** behaviour

---

PAPER 27 **(1)** WISE **(2)** 326 **(3)** pheasant **(4)** phrase **(5)** phial **(6)** orphan **(7)** shoot **(8)** 14 **(9)** (D) **(10)** 24 **(11)** straighten **(12)** Cruelty **(13)** MOIST **(14)** pie **(15)** cake **(16)** GIRAFFE **(17)** moult **(18)** worry **(19)** litter **(20)** hideous **(21)** drizzle **(22)** industrious **(23)** harmony **(24)** fuselage **(25)** railway **(26)** footpath, pavement **(27)** sauce **(28)** cooking

---

PAPER 28 **(1)** MAKE A PRETENCE OR LIKENESS **(2)** 1965 **(3)** 20th **(4)** dialogue **(5)** monologue **(6)** catalogue **(7)** fleet **(8)** 6 **(9)** (A) **(10)** $\frac{4}{7}$ **(11)** fleeing **(12)** England **(13)** 256 **(14)** TOPIC **(15)** hornet's **(16)** sardines **(17)** WASHINGTON **(18)** gaunt **(19)** gourd **(20)** cape **(21)** visible **(22)** simultaneous, simultaneously **(23)** doze **(24)** retain **(25)** chariot **(26)** green **(27)** orange **(28)** studying

---

PAPER 29 **(1)** PLENTIFUL **(2)** (D) **(3)** examine **(4)** tambourine **(5)** magazine **(6)** ogre **(7)** 32 **(8)** (D) **(9)** 26 **(10)** declines **(11)** Peace **(12)** 8 or 15 **(13)** WISE **(14)** crocodile **(15)** horse **(16)** BRADMAN **(17)** heap **(18)** caulk **(19)** scales **(20)** fatal **(21)** ambition **(22)** plumage **(23)** humane **(24)** NASA **(25)** distil **(26)** fighting

---

GENERAL KNOWLEDGE

(1) Kipling **(2)** Verne **(3)** Twain **(4)** Carroll **(5)** Grahame **(6)** Tolkien **(7)** Barrie **(8)** Milne **(9)** Dickens **(10)** Barnard **(11)** Laennec **(12)** Lister **(13)** Jenner **(14)** Salk **(15)** Fleming **(16)** Roentgen **(17)** Mesmer **(18)** Marx **(19)** Caesar **(20)** Einstein **(21)** Hannibal **(22)** Parkes **(23)** Daimler **(24)** Pavlova **(25)** Wright **(26)** Rommel **(27)** Nightingale **(28)** Tutankhamen **(29)** Montezuma **(30)** Bell **(31)** Napoleon **(32)** Magellan **(33)** Galileo **(34)** Hitler **(35)** Gandhi **(36)** Fawkes **(37)** Cleopatra **(38)** Melba **(39)** Drake

---

Coroneos Publications – Titles by Topic
BASIC SKILLS SERIES

ISBN	Item	Title	Author
Basic Skills Maths Tests			
9781862941076	42	Further Maths Tests for Selective Schools Scholarship Exams Yrs 5–8	Coroneos, An, Smith
9781862940697	49	Maths Tests for Selective Schools Scholarship Exams Yrs 5–8	Coroneos, An, Smith
Basic Skills Tests			
9781862941243	112	Further Selective Schools Scholarship Tests Multiple Choice Yrs 5–8	Peter Howard
9781862941359	125	Year/Grade 4 Tests (O.C.) Multiple choice Yrs 4–5	Peter Howard
9781862940598	64	Selective Schools Scholarship Tests Yrs 5–8	Peter Howard
9781862940758	73	Basic Skills Test Yrs 3–8 - Suitable preparation for NAPLAN Tests	Peter Howard
9781862941403	144	Year 3 Basic Skills Test - Suitable preparation for NAPLAN Tests	Peter Howard
9781862941632	153	Year 5 Basic Skills Test - Suitable preparation for NAPLAN Tests	Peter Howard
NAPLAN* Format Practice Tests			
9781921565434	235	Language Conventions Year 3 - NAPLAN* Format Practice Tests	Don Robens
9781921565441	236	Language Conventions Year 5 - NAPLAN* Format Practice Tests	Don Robens
9781921565533	245	Language Conventions Year 7 - NAPLAN* Format Practice Tests	Don Robens
9781921565458	237	Writing Year 3 - NAPLAN* Format Practice Tests	Alfred Fletcher
9781921565465	238	Writing Year 5 - NAPLAN* Format Practice Tests	Alfred Fletcher
9781921565519	243	Writing Year 7 - NAPLAN* Format Practice Tests	Alfred Fletcher
9781921565526	244	Writing Year 9 - NAPLAN* Format Practice Tests	Alfred Fletcher
9781921565472	239	Reading Year 3 - NAPLAN* Format Practice Tests	Alfred Fletcher
9781921565489	240	Reading Year 5 - NAPLAN* Format Practice Tests	Alfred Fletcher
9781921565557	247	Reading Year 7- NAPLAN* Format Practice Tests	Alfred Fletcher
9781921565496	241	Numeracy Year 3 - NAPLAN* Format Practice Tests	Don Robens
9781921565502	242	Numeracy Year 5 - NAPLAN* Format Practice Tests	Don Robens
9781921565540	246	Numeracy Year 7 - NAPLAN* Format Practice Tests	Don Robens
Basic Skills General Ability			
9781862942868	176	Giant Book of General Ability Tests Yrs 5–8	Graeme Wilson
9781862940857	81	General Aptitude Tests for Selective Yrs 5–8	Peter Howard
9781862941724	154	IQ Examples Level 1 Yrs 3–4	Peter Howard
9781862941731	155	IQ Examples Level 2 Yrs 5–8	Peter Howard
9781862940727	70	Learn to Think Level 1 Yrs 2–7	Peter Howard
9781862940734	71	Learn to Think Level 2 Yrs 5–8	Peter Howard
Basic Skills Language and Maths			
9781862940635	50	Kindergarten	Peter Howard
9781862940475	51	Year 1 Language/Mathematics	Peter Howard
9781862940482	52	Year 2 Language/Mathematics	Peter Howard
9781862940499	53	Year 3 Language/Mathematics	Peter Howard
9781862940505	54	Year 4 Language/Mathematics	Peter Howard
9781862940512	55	Year 5 Language/Mathematics	Peter Howard
9781862940529	56	Year 6 Language/Mathematics	Peter Howard
9781862940765	74	Year 7 Language/Mathematics	Peter Howard
9781862940864	82	Year 8 Language/Mathematics	Peter Howard
9781862941274	117	Maths & Language Problems Level 1 Yrs 1–2	Peter Howard
9781862941281	118	Maths & Language Problems Level 2 Yrs 5–8	Peter Howard
9781862941298	119	Maths & Language Problems Level 1 Yrs 1–2	Peter Howard
9781862941564	146	Challenging Maths Problems Yrs 5–8	
Basic Skills Maths			
9781862940642	65	Basic Skills Maths Level 1 Yrs 1–2	Peter Howard
9781862940659	66	Basic Skills Maths Level 2 Yrs 3–4	Peter Howard
9781862940666	67	Basic Skills Maths Level 3 Yrs 5–8	Peter Howard
9781862940994	95	Practice & Improve Your Maths Yr K–1	Arthur Baillie
9781862941007	96	Practice & Improve Your Maths Yr 2	Arthur Baillie
9781862941014	97	Practice & Improve Your Maths Yr 3	Arthur Baillie
9781862941021	98	Practice & Improve Your Maths Yr 4	Arthur Baillie
9781862941038	99	Practice & Improve Your Maths Yr 5	Arthur Baillie
9781862941045	100	Practice & Improve Your Maths Yr 6	Arthur Baillie
Easy Learn Maths			
9781862942844	145A	Basic Skills Easy– Learn Maths Pre/Kinder A	Valerie Marett
9781862942851	145B	Basic Skills Easy– Learn Maths Pre/Kinder B	Valerie Marett
9781862941410	130	Basic Skills Easy– Learn Maths 1A	Julin Tan
9781862941427	131	Basic Skills Easy– Learn Maths 1B	Julin Tan
9781862941434	132	Basic Skills Easy– Learn Maths 2A	Julin Tan

Coroneos Publications – Titles by Topic

Coroneos Publications – Titles by Topic

Basic Skills Fun Learning

9781862941748	156	Fun Learning Activity Book 1 Ages 3–5	Peter Howard
9781862941755	157	Fun Learning Activity Book 2 Ages 6–8	Peter Howard
9781862941762	158	Fun Learning Activity Book3 Ages 9–11	Peter Howard
9781862941335	123	Oz Slang All Ages	Peter Howard
9781862942141	204	More Oz Slang	Peter Howard

Basic Skills Early Years

9781862941342	124	Introductory Comprehension Yrs K–3	Peter Howard
9781862941373	127	Pre-School Activities 1	Peter Howard
9781862941380	128	Pre-School Activities 2	Peter Howard
9781862940703	68	Reading Practice Yrs 1–3	Peter Howard
9781862940772	75	My First Reading 1000 Reading/Spelling Words yrs K–3	Peter Howard
9781862940819	77	Fun with Words Book 1 (colour) Yrs K–3	Peter Howard
9781862940826	78	Fun with Words Book 2 (colour) Yrs K–3	Peter Howard
9781862940833	79	Counting Practice Yrs K and Under	Peter Howard
9781862940840	80	First Reading Yrs k and Under	Peter Howard
9781862940932	89	First Creative Writing Yrs K–3	Peter Howard
9781862940949	90	Picture words Yrs K and under	Peter Howard
9781862941212	111	First Phonics Yrs K–3	Peter Howard
9781862941229	113	First phonic reading Yrs K–3	Peter Howard
9781862941236	114	Introductory Creative Writing Yrs K–3	Peter Howard
9781862941250	115	First Words Yrs K–3	Peter Howard
9781862941304	120	Second words Yrs K–3	Peter Howard
9781862940871	83	First handwriting Yrs K–2	Peter Howard
9781862940888	84	Handwriting Practice Yrs 3–4	Peter Howard

Early Basic Skills NSW font

9781921565564	266	Early Basic Skills Single Sounds – using NSW font	D.J. Ferguson
9781921565571	267	Early Basic Skills Simple Words & Sentences – using NSW font	D.J. Ferguson
9781921565588	268	Early Basic Skills Blending Consonants – using NSW font	D.J. Ferguson
9781921565595	269	Early Basic Skills Using Digraphs – using NSW font	D.J. Ferguson
9781921565601	270	Early Basic Skills Written Text – Punctuation & Grammar – using NSW font	D.J. Ferguson

Early Basic Skills Victorian font

9781921565618	366	Early Basic Skills Single Sounds – using Victorian font	D.J. Ferguson
9781921565625	367	Early Basic Skills Simple Words & Sentences – using Victorian font	D.J. Ferguson
9781921565632	368	Early Basic Skills Blending Consonants – using Victorian font	D.J. Ferguson
9781921565649	369	Early Basic Skills Using Digraphs – using Victorian font	D.J. Ferguson
9781921565656	370	Early Basic Skills Written Text – Punctuation & Grammar – using Victorian font	D.J. Ferguson

Early Basic Skills Queensland font

9781921565793	466	Early Basic Skills Single Sounds – using Queensland font	D.J. Ferguson
9781921565809	467	Early Basic Skills Simple Words & Sentences – using Queensland font	D.J. Ferguson
9781921565816	468	Early Basic Skills Blending Consonants – using Queensland font	D.J. Ferguson
9781921565823	469	Early Basic Skills Using Digraphs – using Queensland font	D.J. Ferguson
9781921565830	470	Early Basic Skills Written Text – Punctuation & Grammar – using Queensland font	D.J. Ferguson

Early Learning Skills (old editions)

9781862941779	166	Early Learning Skills Book 1 Pre School/Kinder - Single Sounds	Denise Tyras
9781862941786	167	Early Learning Skills Book 2 Years K–1 - Three Letter Words	Denise Tyras
9781862941793	168	Early Learning Skills Book 3 Years 1–2 - Blends	Denise Tyras
9781862941854	172	Grammar, Punctuation and Vocabulary Years 1/2	Denise Tyras

DON ROBENS TITLES

Spelling

9781862941946	188	Spelling Year 1	Don Robens
9781862941953	189	Spelling Year 2	Don Robens
9781862941960	190	Spelling Year 3	Don Robens
9781862941977	191	Spelling Year 4	Don Robens
9781862941984	192	Spelling Year 5	Don Robens
9781862941991	193	Spelling Year 6	Don Robens

Creative Writing

9781862942028	196	Writing in Text Types Year 3	Don Robens
9781862942035	197	Writing in Text Types Year 4	Don Robens
9781862942042	198	Writing in Text Types Year 5	Don Robens
9781862942059	199	Writing in Text Types Year 6	Don Robens

Comprehension

9781921565755	248	Comprehension Year 3	Don Robens
9781921565762	249	Comprehension Year 4	Don Robens
9781921565779	250	Comprehension Year 5	Don Robens
9781921565786	251	Comprehension Year 6	Don Robens

AUSTRALIAN HOMESCHOOLING

English

9781862942219	510	Successful English 1	Valerie Marett
9781862942226	511	Successful English 2	Valerie Marett
9781862942479	512	Successful English 3A	Valerie Marett
9781862942486	513	Successful English 3B	Valerie Marett
9781921565250	527	Successful English 4A	Valerie Marett
9781921565267	528	Successful English 4B	Valerie Marett
9781921565342	536	Successful English 5A	Valerie Marett
9781921565359	537	Successful English 5B	Valerie Marett
9781922034076	547	Successful English 6A	Valerie Marett
9781922034083	548	Successful English 6B	Valerie Marett
9781922034199	558	Successful English 7A	Valerie Marett
9781922034205	559	Successful English 7B	Valerie Marett

Spelling

9781862942233	514	Successful Spelling K	Valerie Marett
9781862942240	515	Successful Spelling 1	Valerie Marett
9781862942257	516	Successful Spelling 2	Valerie Marett
9781862942493	517	Successful Spelling 3	Valerie Marett
9781921565304	532	Successful Spelling 4	Valerie Marett
9781921565663	538	Successful Spelling 5	Valerie Marett
9781862942837	177	Learn to Read, Write & Spell 1 – Yrs K–1	Valerie Marett
9781862942820	178	Learn to Read, Write & Spell 2 – Yrs K–1	Valerie Marett
9781862942769	179	Learn to Read, Write & Spell 3 – Yrs 1–3	Valerie Marett
9781862942776	180	Learn to Read, Write & Spell 4 – Yrs 1–3	Valerie Marett
9781862942783	181	Learn to Read, Write & Spell 5 – Yrs 1–4	Valerie Marett
9781862942790	182	Learn to Read, Write & Spell 6 – Yrs 3–8	Valerie Marett
9781862942806	183	Learn to Read, Write & Spell 7 – Yrs 5–10	Valerie Marett

Mathematics

9781862942158	501	Learning Multiplication 1 – Australian Homeschooling	Carmel Musumeci
9781862942165	502	Learning Multiplication 2 – Australian Homeschooling	Carmel Musumeci
9781921565298	531	Practise Your Addition and Subtraction to 20	Marett & Musumeci

Phonics

9781921565229	524	Revise Your Phonics 1	Valerie Marett
9781921565236	525	Revise Your Phonics 2	Valerie Marett

Social Studies HSIE / SOSE

9781862942509	503	Succeeding in Social Studies K	Valerie Marett
9781862942516	504	Succeeding in Social Studies 1	Valerie Marett
9781862942523	505	Succeeding in Social Studies 2	Valerie Marett
9781862942530	506	Succeeding in Social Studies 3	Valerie Marett
9781862942547	507	Succeeding in Social Studies 4	Valerie Marett
9781862942554	508	Succeeding in Social Studies 5	Valerie Marett
9781862942561	509	Succeeding in Social Studies 6	Valerie Marett
9781921565212	523	Australian History 1901–1945	Valerie Marett
9781921565335	535	Australian Government	Valerie Marett
9781922034175	556	Understanding Geography	Valerie Marett

Science

9781921565694	541	Secondary Science 7A – General Science	Frank Marett
9781921565700	542	Secondary Science 7B – Biology	Frank Marett
9781921565724	544	Secondary Science 7C – Earth and Space	Frank Marett
9781921565717	543	Secondary Science 8A – Matter and Energy	Frank Marett
9781921565748	546	Secondary Science 8B – The Body	Frank Marett
9781922034144	557	Secondary Science 8C – Geology	Frank Marett
9781921565731	545	Secondary Science 9A – Chemistry	Frank Marett
9781922034137	555	Secondary Science 9C – Environmental Science	Frank Marett

Testing

9781862942172	518	Test your Maths K–1	Valerie Marett
9781862942189	519	Test Your Maths 2	Valerie Marett

Coroneos Publications – Titles by Topic

MATHEMATICS

Secondary Texts

Past Papers and Solutions

Past Papers and Solutions (Older Series)

Practice (Specimen) Papers

Study Skills